The Country Road Through The Book Of
Matthew

≈

Mike Lovett

Copyright © 2016 Kenneth M. Lovett

All rights reserved. No part of this book may be used or reproduced by any means, graphic, electronic, or mechanical, including photocopying, recording, taping or by any information storage retrieval system without the written permission of the author except in the case of brief quotations embodied in critical articles and reviews.

This book is a work of non-fiction. Unless otherwise noted, the author and the publisher make no explicit guarantees as to the accuracy of the information contained in this book and in some cases, names of people and places have been altered to protect their privacy.

Scripture quotations are taken from the Holy Bible, New Living Translation, copyright © 1996, 2004, 2007, 2013 by Tyndale House Foundation. Used by permission of Tyndale House Publishers, Inc., Carol Stream, Illinois 60188. All rights reserved.

Because of the dynamic nature of the Internet, any web addresses or links contained in this book may have changed since publication and may no longer be valid.

ISBN: 978-0-9977551-2-1 (sc)
ISBN: 978-0-9977551-3-8 (e)

Library of Congress Control Number: 2016911526

Revision Date 08/01/2016

To Caroline,

My beloved wife and faithful partner in ministry

Contents

~ Introduction ~ 1

~ 1 ~ 5
~ 2 ~ 7
~ 3 ~ 13
~ 4 ~ 15
~ 5 ~ 21
~ 6 ~ 34
~ 7 ~ 43
~ 8 ~ 52
~ 9 ~ 60
~ 10 ~ 72
~ 11 ~ 81
~ 12 ~ 89
~ 13 ~ 99
~ 14 ~ 110
~ 15 ~ 117
~ 16 ~ 123
~ 17 ~ 129
~ 18 ~ 135
~ 19 ~ 141
~ 20 ~ 146
~ 21 ~ 152
~ 22 ~ 160

~ 23 ~	168
~ 24 ~	178
~ 25 ~	188
~ 26 ~	191
~ 27 ~	206
~ 28 ~	218
~ What's Next? ~	223

~ Introduction ~

When I was young, my family would take road trips whenever the opportunity presented itself. My parents would pack us up and we would be off on another adventure in the newest rebuilt road machine assembled by my dad. Destinations included, state parks, relatives' homes, and out of the way picnic areas. And although the interstate highway system was well under way by then, it usually wasn't going where we were. No, you were more likely to catch us on some narrow two-lane country road than a four lane super-highway that promised quick trips with no stops. But, as they say, getting there was half the fun.

We would stop at roadside watermelon stands for a cooling snack. Sometimes, we would pull into a travel stop to scope out the latest in souvenirs. Sandy creeks that crossed under wooden bridges made great rest stops. And anything crossing the road on four legs was an opportunity to stop and learn more about nature. Sometimes gravel, occasionally blacktop, but always dusty, the back roads and byways that made up many of our routes were designed for discovery. Often they were lined with berry bushes that begged to be picked or sugar cane gleanings that were just right to sweeten the day.

You could get where you were going a lot faster on the interstate, but it was harder to roll the windows down and enjoy the fragrances along the way. On the country road, we would open every window and breathe in the honeysuckle, fresh cut hay, or approaching rain, even if it was interrupted by the occasional skunk or fresh cow patty. And the sound of cicada, crickets, and bullfrogs during an evening drive was music that could never be replicated by the FM radio. Fireflies at night, glimpses of deer in the side throw of the headlights, and shooting stars marked the long drives home after the sun had made its daily farewell.

The interstate was made to be fast. The country road was made to be slow. The interstate got you to your destination, but with little enjoyment. The country road took a little longer, but you were left with an appreciation of where you had been. The interstate cut out a part of our lives that we thought we would never miss, but realize now that we have.

The same is true for our study of God's word. In today's fast paced get-it-done-and-move-on-to-the-next-thing society we leave little time for the slow study of God's scriptures. Give it to us fast, let us read it fast, make your point fast, so that we can move on to the next step in our relationship with Him. Churches left and right are shaving sermons more as our attention spans become less. In our quest to get there fast we have left the appreciation of the relationship in the dust. God's Word is not a "how to" book. It is a "how are you?" book. It is a "do you know me?" book. It is not enough to simply commit it to memory. We need to take the time to listen to it, to feel it, to breathe it in, and to appreciate where it has been and where it can take us.

This book is designed to do just that. It is designed to slow us down so that we can experience God's word in our own lives. Paul told Timothy that,

"All Scripture is inspired by God and is useful to teach us what is true and to make us realize what is wrong in our lives. It corrects us when we are wrong and teaches us to do what is right. God uses it to prepare and equip His people to do every good work." (2 Timothy 3:16, 17 NLT)

Did you catch the first two words in that statement? Paul said *all scripture* is inspired and useful. How often do we rush through what we think are transitional portions of the bible, just so we can get to what we think are the major themes quicker? And what do we miss when we do that? Every scripture in the book of Matthew is used in these pages. I encourage you to only examine one section (not chapter) each day. Read the verses several times as you meditate on their meaning. Take the devotional and allow it to stir your own thoughts as you prayerfully ask the Holy Spirit to breathe life into the words. Pray about the things you are dealing with in your own life. Ask

God to show you how daily reading lends guidance in those situations. And please, please, please, never read this book without your Bible and a pencil handy! As you listen to Jesus speaking to you through the scriptures, write down what is revealed. Use the margins of this book if necessary, or a notebook if it is available. Never underestimate the power of journaling your time with God.

Take the time to drink in the images of the stable in Bethlehem. Listen to the gulls as Jesus teaches along the shores of Galilee. Hear the agony of the woman with the issue. Watch the joy of the blind beggars made to see. Experience the heartache of Peter after his denial. Feel the earth beneath your feet as you follow Jesus from Nazareth to Jerusalem and back again. Imagine yourself as the child on Jesus' lap, or a disciple embarrassed for arguing about who is the best. Take time to take it all in. The road to faster learning is wide, and there are a lot of people on it. But the road to better learning is narrow, and few people venture down it anymore. So as we begin our journey through the book of Matthew I ask that you consider taking your time. I pray that you will stop and learn along the way. I hope that you will not give in to the urge to get through it quick. And I encourage you to allow God to speak to your heart as we step out onto the country road…

~ 1 ~

This is a record of the ancestors of Jesus the Messiah, a descendant of David and of Abraham – Matthew 1:1 (NLT)

Read Matthew 1:1-17

As we enter the gospel of Matthew, the first thing we read is a genealogy of the human family of Jesus. The Jews kept meticulous ancestral records and, to this day, claim to be able to trace their family trees back to ancient times. And so it was with some confidence that Matthew was able to proclaim the roots from which Jesus' family tree grew. Matthew wrote his gospel to show the Jews of his day how the person of Jesus fulfilled the prophecies of the Old Testament concerning the arrival of the Messiah. As we make our way through these pages, I pray that we will not miss the significance of both the number of prophesies that came to pass in His life as well as the accuracy with which they were carried out. As we begin our journey, let's see why it was important that the Jews recognized what was happening and how it is essential for us to recognize what happened as well.

~

When Joseph woke up, he did as the angel of the Lord commanded and took Mary as his wife. -Matthew 1:24 (NLT)

Read Matthew 1:18-25

Joseph was a good and devout man. He knew what the penalty would be for Mary if it became known that she was pregnant outside of marriage. Joseph was trying to handle the situation in a way that spared her as much as possible. But, Joseph could only see the human side of things and was not aware of the story unfolding in the heavenly realm. It took angelic revelation for him to know his, Mary's, and Jesus' place in prophecy. But once he was aware of God's plan, Joseph did not waver from his purpose. There will be times in our lives when things just do not make sense to us. But if we remain in God's word and stay true to His Son, we too will receive guidance from the Holy Spirit about the steps to take in our own situations. Then, like Joseph, we can move forward, knowing that our course is sure.

~ 2 ~

About that time some wise men from eastern lands arrived in Jerusalem, asking, "Where is the newborn king of the Jews? We saw his star as it rose, and we have come to worship him." – Matthew 2:1, 2 (NLT)

Read Matthew 2:1-8

The wise men were scholars from the area surrounding Babylon. They had grown up studying the writings of Daniel, the Old Testament prophet who once lived there in exile. The wise men had devoted their lives to finding the Messiah. When the time was right and the prophecies were coming true, they were able to recognize the signs and were ready to move to see the new King. On the other hand, Herod and the people of Jerusalem were not even looking for the Messiah. Aside from a devoted few, they were too busy with daily life. As heirs of the promise, they knew the Messiah would come one day; but they expected Him to arrive with fanfare and self-proclamation so they missed His arrival completely. The same can be true for us if we are not careful. Most of us know of Jesus. Even if we have never been in a church, we have heard about whom He claimed to be and what He did on earth. However, the only way we will know Jesus is if we seek Him with our whole heart. If we chase after Him as the wise men did, by reading the scriptures and spending time in prayer, Jesus will reveal Himself to us. But if, like the people of Jerusalem, we choose to go about our daily life and hope that He will show up and announce His presence, we will miss the greatest gift of all. So let's take up the chase with all we have. The effort may be more than we can stand at times, but the reward will be more than we can imagine.

They entered the house and saw the child with his mother, Mary, and they bowed down and worshiped him. —Matthew 2:11 (NLT)

Read Matthew 2:9-12

The wise men were interested in one thing; finding and worshipping the King of the Jews. Because they stayed true to that one desire and completed their mission, their reward was the very thing that they sought. If we stay true to our own pursuit of Christ, we too will receive what we seek. Not only will we find what we seek, but God will also protect us from those who would interfere, just as He protected the wise men from those who would have kept them from their goal. When we give up the right to guide our own lives and place our path in His hands, we may be surprised, but we will never be disappointed.

~

"Get up! Flee to Egypt with the child and his mother," the angel said. "Stay there until I tell you to return, because Herod is going to search for the child to kill him." —Matthew 2:13 (NLT)

Read Matthew 2:13-15

When we operate in God's will by obeying His commandments and listening to His words, He will keep us on the path to fulfill His objectives. Will it always be easy? Of course not! Imagine Joseph, faced with the prospect of packing up in the middle of the night, with a wife and child, and heading to a country he knew nothing about. The same can be said of Abraham (who also went in search of a country), Moses (who led a nation out of Egypt), or David (who waited forty years to be the king). Nevertheless, when it makes no sense to us, God has a reason and that reason usually involves our growing in faith. God also offers protection from a fate worse than anything we may see ahead. When we stay in His will and listen for His voice, we enjoy the protection of the One who is able to see all, do all, and to stop all those who would harm His children.

~

Herod's brutal action fulfilled what God had spoken through the prophet Jeremiah: "A cry was heard in Ramah— weeping and great mourning. Rachel weeps for her children, refusing to be comforted, for they are dead." - Matthew 2:17, 18 (NLT)

Read Matthew 2:16-18

Why does God let bad things happen to good people? That is not a question which I am qualified to answer. Do not let anyone else convince you that they are either, because the truth is no one will really know "Why?" until they reach heaven. For reasons known only to God, Satan has been allowed to temporarily rule over this earth. Those who follow him, like Herod, commit evil acts every day. From our perspective, it can seem unfair that some people are protected while others are not. However, when we stop to think about where innocents go once they have suffered evil, we can have faith that the Father truly loves and cares for His children. For those who are struggling with the question of "Why?" the only answer is to take comfort in knowing that God is in control, and that whatever His reasons are, they are perfect. Even if they don't make sense to us right now.

~

So the family went and lived in a town called Nazareth. This fulfilled what the prophets had said: "He will be called a Nazarene." - Matthew 2: 23 (NLT)

Read Matthew 2:19-23

People who have searched the Old Testament prophecies about the coming Messiah must have been confused at times. Some prophecies said He would come from Bethlehem, while others said He would be called a Nazarene. How could both be true? Yet, God is always able to bring about that which He said would happen through ways we would never have guessed. The same is true for us today. Do you find yourself in a situation where the promises of God in scripture seem unattainable? Do not worry. God specializes in the impossible! Simply follow Him, hang onto His Son, and learn from His words. Through faith in the Father, we will arrive at His promises, even if we have to go to Egypt and back to get there.

~ 3 ~

The prophet Isaiah was speaking about John when he said, "He is a voice shouting in the wilderness, 'Prepare the way for the Lord's coming! Clear the road for him!'" - Matthew 3:3 (NLT)

Read Matthew 3:1-12

The story of John the Baptist takes up so little room in the Bible, yet arguably he had the most important role in human history; heralding the arrival of the Messiah. In our lives as well, we may be called into Serving God in ways that, while important to the Kingdom, will never be celebrated here on earth. Let us not concern ourselves with the accolades of the world. Instead, let us be faithful to move forward in the work that God has placed in front of each of us. Regardless of what we are called to do, let us remember that anything asked of us in the advancement of God's Kingdom has importance beyond our imagination. My prayer is that when we are called, we will answer with the same dedication as John.

But Jesus said, "It should be done, for we must carry out all that God requires." —Matthew 3:15 (NLT)

Read Matthew 3:13-17

In this day and age when people are told they are answerable to no one but themselves, Jesus stands out as a counter culture example. Even though He was the chosen Messiah, He held Himself accountable to God and obeyed the same scriptures that you and I read today. Even when others, such as John, tried to give Him a pass, He insisted on doing the right thing. I pray that we too would follow the precepts found in God's Word. Not because salvation lies in being good enough, but because we love the Father and want to please Him. He has given us everything through Christ. So is our obedience too much to ask? If Christ, being perfect, found it necessary to submit Himself to the Father's will, should we not obey God as well? The choice is ours; but God's own words make it clear. He loves those who obey Him.

~ 4 ~

"Get out of here, Satan," Jesus told him. "For the Scriptures say, 'You must worship the Lord your God and serve only him.'" –Matthew 4:10 (NLT)

Read Matthew 4:1-11

Have you ever been tempted to take something that is not yours because you were in need? How about to test God because you were not sure He really exists? Has anyone ever tried to convince you to do something you knew was wrong by offering you some grand reward? Good news! You have something in common with Jesus. The scriptures tell us that Jesus was tempted in the same ways that we are tempted. However, there is one difference; Jesus never sinned. How was He able to resist the temptation? Today's passage is the key. For each temptation He faced, Jesus knew scriptures that answered the temptation.

The bible is referred to as a sword for this very reason. If we study it, bury its verses in our hearts, and remember those verses in times of temptation, then we will be able to defend ourselves when Satan attacks. The temptation will pass without sin on our part. Will we wield our sword as perfectly as Jesus did while He was on earth? Of course not! Nevertheless, we should still use the bible to the best of our ability. Hear the good news. Because Jesus was tempted in every way, He is able to go to the Father on our behalf when we fail and say, "Please have mercy. I faced that temptation too and I know how hard it is to deal with." Since He never succumbed to temptation, Jesus was able to take the penalty for all of our failures to resist temptation. In these verses we see that Jesus did leave us the secret to thwarting temptation. Let us begin today to read, memorize, and recall God's word so that we too can defend ourselves with the sharpest sword in God's Kingdom. .

This fulfilled what God said through the prophet Isaiah: "In the land of Zebulun and of Naphtali, beside the sea, beyond the Jordan River, in Galilee where so many Gentiles live, the people who sat in darkness have seen a great light. And for those who lived in the land where death casts its shadow, a light has shined." —Matthew 4:14-16 (NLT)

Read Matthew 4:12-17

For the religious leaders who knew the prophecies of the Old Testament, the credibility of Jesus as Messiah should have been clear. Yet, most of that group of people was in darkness about His sovereignty. Even today, there are people who know the Bible, but still do not know Jesus. But His light does shine among those who are earnestly and honestly seeking Him with their whole heart. Until that moment though, we may as well be trying to read the bible with the lights turned off. The apostle Paul said, *"Whenever someone turns to the Lord, the veil is taken away. For the Lord is the Spirit, and wherever the Spirit of the Lord is, there is freedom. So all of us who have had that veil removed can see and reflect the glory of the Lord."* (2 Corinthians: 16, 17 NLT). Let us seek Christ with all of our being, so that just as it did for the Gentiles of old, the Light of the world will shine in, and out, of our hearts today.

~

Jesus called out to them, "Come, follow me, and I will show you how to fish for people!" –Matthew 4:19 (NLT)

Read Matthew 4:18-22

When Jesus went looking for disciples, He did not go to the temple or to the synagogue. He was not searching for preachers, theologians, or even educated men. He sought out ordinary people that He could teach and work through to start His church to spread the gospel throughout the earth. Fishermen, a tax collector, and guys just hanging out on the corner (or under a tree), were chosen to lead the original church. Why? Because God chooses to work through vessels willing to allow God to receive the glory. Years after the first disciples were chosen, the Holy Spirit came to live in them. The disciples began to preach and teach and perform miracles. People asked how men of their backgrounds could do such things and many rightly concluded that only God could be responsible. As a result, many believed in the gospel of Jesus Christ and the church grew. Even today, God still looks for those who would follow Him. God looks for those ready to do His will so that He will receive the glory, people will believe in Jesus, and accept what He did for them on the cross. God is not looking for degrees, or experience, or even stature, but open hearts. Has He found you on the lakeshore yet? My prayer is that if He has not found you yet, He soon will.

~

News about him spread as far as Syria, and people soon began bringing to him all who were sick. And whatever their sickness or disease, or if they were demon possessed or epileptic or paralyzed—he healed them all. — Matthew 4:24

Read Matthew 4:23-25

From the beginning of His ministry, people have come to Jesus to learn, learning, to be healed, and for salvation. What was true then is still true today. Only those who come to Him will find what they need to be whole again. Why? Because no matter where we turn, we will never find anything to fill the void in our hearts that only He can fill. There is no joy like that of the person who discovers Jesus on a personal level. Whatever our needs, Jesus is the answer. He can take care of whatever we face. He will never disappoint and we will never walk alone again.

~ 5 ~

One day as he saw the crowds gathering, Jesus went up on the mountainside and sat down. His disciples gathered around him, and he began to teach them. —Matthew 5:1, 2 (NLT)

Read Matthew 5:1-10

What does God honor? Virtues like humility, charity, peacefulness, righteousness, justice, purity, and mercy. Jesus taught that God would bless people who demonstrated these qualities. We now know these qualities as fruits of the spirit. We also understand that we grow stronger in these virtues as we grow in Christ. People in Jesus' day did not know about the crucifixion, the resurrection, or the in dwelling of the Holy Spirit in believers yet, so Jesus presented the same ideas to them in ways that they could understand. As He prepared them for the coming kingdom, Jesus taught them things they would understand better, once His mission had been completed. God has blessed us to live in an age where we have that completed mission as part of our history. Therefore, we understand how we should respond to the gospel message. As we grow in our faith, I pray that we continue to grow in the qualities that mark us as true believers as well.

~

"And remember, the ancient prophets were persecuted in the same way." – Matthew 5:12 (NLT)

Read Matthew 5:11, 12

Have you experienced persecution for following Christ? In this country, we may not fear for our lives because of our beliefs, but we can be mistreated, ostracized, and discriminated against for them. Have you been passed over for a promotion? Have you been denied a special project at work? Have you been ridiculed at school, or left out of a social circle because of your faith? Jesus says to be glad when these things happen to us, because we will be rewarded. Though it may seem far off to us now, we will soon forget the temporary struggles we suffered through as part of life on earth.

I pray that we keep Christ's promise in front of us as we demonstrate His love to others. Before long, eternally speaking, we will be enjoying the rewards that come from faithfulness while here on earth. It sounds like we will be doing so in pretty fair company.

~

"You are the salt of the earth. But what good is salt if it has lost its flavor?" –Matthew 5:13 (NLT)

Read Matthew 5:13-16

Why do we salt our food? So we may change its flavor. Why do we turn on a light? So we may change the condition of a room. Why do we follow Christ in a visible way? So He may change those who see us. You do know that people, who watch true followers, are always changed, don't you? Whether we see it or not, those who witness Christ in action through His disciples are forever changed. People see the gospel in action and have to decide what to do with the information they have received. Will they always make the right decision with this new information? No, not always. But that does not change the fact that they have witnessed the behavior of a believer. So keep shaking the salt, keep shining the light, and keep demonstrating Christ, in word and in deed. For just like salt that loses it flavor and light that is hidden, believers who do not share what they have lose their usefulness in the kingdom. We may all be called to witness in different manners, but we are all called to witness. May all of us find a way today to spice up someone else's life with the gospel of Jesus Christ.

~

"I did not come to abolish the law of Moses or the writings of the prophets. No, I came to accomplish their purpose." —Matthew 5:17 (NLT)

Read Matthew 5:17-20

If we took the entire book of the law and boiled it down to its basic idea, it is this: In order to be found righteous before God, you cannot sin, not even once. If you do sin, then a sacrifice has to be made to cover that sin. Every time you sin, another sacrifice is required.

If we took the writing of the prophets in its entirety and boiled it down to its basic idea, it is this: Sacrificing animals is an imperfect way to satisfy a perfect God. But One would come who would present people with a perfect way to satisfy a perfect God. Jesus was the perfect sacrifice required by the law and predicted by the prophets. But Jesus warned that even reliance on His sacrifice did not give people a free pass when it came to obeying God. We all make mistakes, but to willfully disobey God is to mock what Jesus did on the cross. Willful disobedience is rebellion against God. And who wants to be in opposition of Him? I pray that we choose instead to obey God, who loved us enough to sacrifice His own Son, in our place, so that we could enter into His presence and eternity.

"You have heard that our ancestors were told, 'You must not murder. If you commit murder, you are subject to judgment.' But I say, if you are even angry with someone, you are subject to judgment!" —Matthew 5:21, 22
(NLT)

Read Matthew 5:21-26

After Israel's diaspora in Babylon, the Jewish religious leaders had rightfully concluded that their exile was the result of sin in the nation. So they took the Mosaic Law and attempted to refine it to the nth degree. For example, they took the command not to work on the Sabbath and defined what constituted work. Walking less than a certain distance was not work while walking more than that distance was. Picking a few heads of wheat to satisfy hunger was considered work as well. The leaders did this with each of the commandments. They attempted to look at every possible situation and define what a violation was and what it was not. Jesus arrived on the scene and told the religious leaders that they had focused on the action, but they had failed to focus on the heart conditions that lie at the base of sin. Hate, greed, pride, and lust, were the real problem and showed themselves in the actions that violated the law. He challenged people to address those sins of the heart. He lays that challenge at our feet as well. So let us examine our own hearts to see what could be leading us down the path to sin. Then we can ask for forgiveness, before the sin that is hidden in our hearts is exposed to the world.

~

"So if your eye—even your good eye —causes you to lust, gouge it out and throw it away. It is better for you to lose one part of your body than for your whole body to be thrown into hell." –Matthew 5:29 (NLT)

Read Matthew 5:27-30

Sin always starts from desires in our hearts that are wrong and each of us has things or situations in our lives that can trigger those desires and cause us to sin. A job that puts us in close proximity with someone of the opposite sex, a television that we let control us instead of the opposite, hobbies that take us places we should not , and would not go otherwise, are just a few examples. While the situation or object itself may not be bad, when it is cause for us to sin, then we should rid ourselves of it as quickly as possible. As Jesus said, it is better to lose something and enter into eternity, than to hang onto our toys, our friends, or our comfort zones, and ride them into hell. We should honestly assess what is going on in our lives and, when we find things that cause us to sin, have the faith and the courage to let them go, knowing that the reward we will receive is much greater than anything we leave behind.

~

"But I say that a man who divorces his wife, unless she has been unfaithful, causes her to commit adultery." –Matthew 5:32 (NLT)

Read Matthew 5:31, 32

Jesus was addressing a real problem. Women were being treated as second-class citizens at best and as property at worst. A man who had grown tired of his wife could simply fill out a piece of paper and be rid of her. Jesus challenged that idea, reminding everyone that two people are involved in a marriage, not just one, and by divorcing his wife without reason, a man was causing his wife to sin as well as himself. When we are about to do something, we should first ask ourselves, "How it will affect others?" Do not forget that Jesus taught us to love others the same way we love ourselves and to treat them in a way that does not cause them to sin. Jesus also taught that marriage is a union of a man and a woman, not a man and his chattel. Two people, joined together in God's eyes forever, whether they choose to honor that marriage or not.

~

Just say a simple, 'Yes, I will,' or 'No, I won't.' Anything beyond this is from the evil one. - Matthew 5:37 NLT

Read Matthew 5:33-37

Why do we make vows anyway? Why is it not good enough to say "yes" or "no"? One reason is pride. We can be so consumed with worry that someone does not believe we are being truthful, that we feel we must add something to our answer that makes it sound more believable. If we are telling the truth, shouldn't that be enough? Let us resist the urge to add to our answer, knowing that our honest reply is all that is required. To do any more is to give in to the sin of pride. And once we give in to the sin of pride, we are no better off than if we had lied in the first place.

~

"Given to those who ask, and don't turn away from those who want to borrow." –Matthew 5:42 (NLT)

Read Matthew 5:38-42

In a world that says take more than you give, Jesus arrives on the scene and says, give and then give some more. You see, if we are to love others as ourselves, then we must give to others, as we would expect them to give to us. Always be ready to give as much as you can, as often as you can. Be ready to give in situations where you will be tempted to take. Remember that no matter how much we give, we will always be on the plus side. For we can never give more than our Heavenly Father has already given to us.

~

"If you love only those who love you, what reward is there for that? Even corrupt tax collectors do that much." —Matthew 5:46 (NLT)

Read Matthew 5:43-48

It is so easy to love those who love us back. That is why anyone can do it. To love those who hate us is a different matter completely. If we are to love our enemies, it takes strength and courage that we can only get from God, who also loves His enemies. Is it a surprise that God loves His enemies? It should not be when we remember that He created all of mankind. So, of course, He loves everyone, even those who break His heart. Are we afraid of having our heart broken? We don't want to get hurt because we love someone who does not love us. It is in those times that we need to remember that God is hurt when His heart is broken too. Nevertheless, He chooses to love anyway, even when we are the ones who have hurt Him. What better example can we have to follow than God, who loved us enough to give up His Son, even as we broke His heart.

~ 6 ~

"Give your gifts in private, and your Father, who sees everything, will reward you." —Matthew 6:4 (NLT)

Read Matthew 6:1-4

Pride is such an insidious emotion. It slips into everything we do with such ease and invisibility that we must be ever on guard against it. Even when we are trying to do for others, Pride will sneak in and steal our reward, if we let it. We must not allow the praise of people to become the driving force of our actions. Allowing the praise of people to drive our actions is the reason Jesus warned us to do our good deeds in secret. He knew how alluring the praise of others can be. It satisfies a basic need to be recognized for what we do. But Christ said if we are satisfied with the praise we receive on Earth, then we give up the praise we are due in Heaven. There will be times when other people learn about the good we have done. But I pray that when they do, we find the strength to humbly deflect any accolade to the Father. After all, it is He who gives us the ability to do good in the first place, so the glory really belongs to Him anyway. And, the best reward we can obtain is the one we receive from Him.

~

"But when you pray, go away by yourself, shut the door behind you, and pray to your Father in private." - Matthew 6:6 (NLT)

Read Matthew 6:5-8

Private prayer is supposed to be just that, private. It is also supposed to be real. God is not interested in rituals. He is interested in a relationship with us. So, find some place that you can be alone with Him and do not be afraid to just talk to Him. He already knows everything that is going on in our lives anyway, so why should we be afraid to open our heart to Him? He will help and guide us. Most of all, He will reveal Himself to us if we take time, to spend time one on one with the One who created us. He already knows us. He just wants us to know Him. What better way to do that than to speak with Him today?

~

"Pray like this: Our Father ..." –Matthew 6:9 (NLT)

Read Matthew 6:9-13

Even though the Lord's Prayer is recited verbatim in church services, Jesus meant the prayer as an outline or guide of how to pray to the Father. We should begin by praising God. Let's praise Him for who He is, what He has done, what He is doing, and what He will do. And while we are praising Him, we should be bold enough to ask that His kingdom would soon replace the prince of the earth and that Jesus' return would not be delayed. Then we should present our needs to Him. Even though He already knows what we need, our faith is strengthened when stated needs are met. Next we intercede for others and forgive those who have wronged us in the same way that we ask God to forgive us. Always pray for protection from the temptations of the devil. And always end by giving Him thanks and praise. As we learned in the prior scripture, God is more interested in us talking to Him in our own words than repeating the exact words out of memory. I pray this morning that we continue in our relationship with the Father by understanding better Jesus' teaching on the most important Christian tool, prayer.

~

"If you forgive those who sin against you, your heavenly Father will forgive you. But if you refuse to forgive others, your Father will not forgive your sins. - Matthew 6:14, 15 NLT

I pray that we can grasp the gravity of Jesus' statement. Our forgiveness is directly connected to our own ability to forgive. Some would argue that Jesus' sacrifice on the cross negates this statement. Others would say that unless we forgive, we have not truly accepted what Christ did for us anyway. I only know that Jesus Himself said, "But if you refuse to forgive others, your Father will not forgive your sins." That's pretty cut and dried. And, lest we be tempted to play word games about what constitutes forgiveness, we may want to remember that God knows our hearts. If we want real forgiveness for our sins, we should be prepared to give real forgiveness to others. Otherwise, we may want to get ready for a long stay in the same prison of resentment in which we keep those we fail to forgive.

~

"And when you fast, don't make it obvious, as the hypocrites do, for they try to look miserable and disheveled so people will admire them for their fasting. I tell you the truth, that is the only reward they will ever get." —Matthew 6:16 (NLT)

Read Matthew 6:16-18

God is not interested in demonstrations designed to garner the admiration of people. He is only interested in the intentions of our hearts. Do we fast so that we can show others how long we can go without food? Or do we fast so that we can use the time we would have spent eating to have interaction with the Father? If it is the latter, then let us show others what a privilege it is to spend time with Him and the joy in our hearts that comes from being in His presence. It is not important that others know about our sacrifices. If we show others anything, let's show them what it really means to be living for the Lord.

~

"Wherever your treasure is, there the desires of your heart will also be." –
Matthew 6:21 (NLT)

Read Matthew 6:19-21

What do you consider important in life? A new car or truck? A piece of jewelry? A certain job? What do you think about throughout the day? What is your focus? What is it that you cannot do without? As we have seen all through His sermon on the mount, Jesus has been addressing matters of the heart. He is not saying it is bad to have "things", only that having them presents the problem of priorities. What are we willing to do to get and keep our stuff? Are we willing to sacrifice our relationship with God and with others to obtain the things we want in this life? Or is that relationship more important than the things we accumulate? The reality is the things we have here in this life will disappear at some point. But our faith in God, our love for Him and our love for those around us, will last through this lifetime and into eternity. Though our faith and love for God and other people may not seem valuable compared to our possessions right now, they are the treasures that really make us rich and prepare us for eternal life with the Father. We should all begin today, while it still is today, to take stock of our treasures and evaluate their worth with heavenly wisdom.

~

"Your eye is a lamp that provides light for your body." —Matthew 6:22 (NLT)

Read Matthew 6:22, 23

So much of who we are comes from the information we hear, and especially, see. If we are not discriminating about what we view, then our mind is going to be filled with information and images that are contrary to whom we should be as Christians. The problem with information that comes in through our eyes is that the mind is able to remind us of that information at either opportune, or inopportune, times without warning. Like film in a camera, images that come in through the shutter of our eyes are forever imprinted on our minds, especially if we expose them to the same thing repeatedly. Those images lay waiting in our minds to be called up by some event that triggers their replay. But just as bad information (darkness) comes in through the eye and is stored in our brain, so does good information (light). The more light we allow in, the more darkness is forced out. So I pray we are careful about where we allow our eyes to go and we avoid areas where a flash is needed.

~

"So don't worry about tomorrow, for tomorrow will bring its own worries. Today's trouble is enough for today." —Matthew 6:34 (NLT)

Read Matthew 6:24-34

Have you ever really given any thought to what you worry about? Most of us worry about things we really cannot control. Things like the weather, wars, or even the global economy. We may worry about things closer to home, such as food for our table, money for our bills, or clothes for our kids. But Jesus called out worry for what it is, a lack of faith. As Christians, we have a Heavenly Father who is more than capable of supplying anything we actually need and He is wise enough to know what we need. Do you not know that everything we have right now is actually His and given to us by Him? So instead of worrying let us focus on the things that spread God's message to others so that they too can begin to worry less. God made us for a reason and He will take care of what we need so let's spread the message we were created to convey and watch our own faith grow as well. And worry will take care of itself.

~ 7 ~

"Do not judge others, and you will not be judged. For you will be treated as you treat others." —Matthew 7:1 (NLT)

Read Matthew 7:1-5

Between witnessing and judging, Christ draws a very thin line and warns us not to cross. We are called to be a lamp and spread the light of God's word. We are not to put ourselves in the place of judge over those who choose not to listen. Why? Because the position of judge is reserved for someone who has never violated the law. I believe I can say with some authority that none of us are qualified on that basis. Until we have dealt with our own sin, we are in no position to deal with the sins of others. So let's use God's Word the way it was intended, as a mirror for our own lives and a light for the lives of others. The Righteous Judge will take care of the rest.

~

"And to everyone who knocks, the door will be opened." —Matthew 7:8
(NLT)

Read Matthew 7:7, 8

Persistent prayer is like a muscle of the Christian faith. The more we persist, the more our faith grows. So we persist more in prayer and grow more in faith and the muscle gets bigger and stronger. Praying engages us in conversation with the Father, no matter the subject of the conversation. God longs to spend time with us in conversation. But the one thing He really wants us to ask Him for is the forgiveness that comes through Christ. That door will be opened to all who ask. So whether you receive what you ask for after one prayer, or one hundred prayers, do not stop praying. God knows what you need, when you need it, and He wants to give you so much more along the way.

"So if you sinful people know how to give good gifts to your children, how much more will your heavenly Father give good gifts to those who ask him."
- Matthew 7:11 (NLT)

Read Matthew 7:9-11

Has there ever been a time when your child asked you for something he or she truly needed, and you did not do everything you could to provide it? Then why would we think that God, the perfect parent, would not do the same thing for us? All we have to do is ask. Just like we, as parents, would determine what is best for our children, God will determine what is best for us. He will decide whether we really need what we are asking for and when we really need it. Then, because nothing is beyond His reach, God will provide. So let's ask for the good gifts that help us to reflect Christ, to spread the message of His saving work, and to help others.

~

"Do to others whatever you would like them to do to you. This is the essence of all that is taught in the law and the prophets." - Matthew 7:12 NLT

Jesus would later rephrase this verse and say "Love your neighbor as yourself." Do we love anyone so much that we would only treat them the way we want to be treated? If so, how long is that list? Jesus challenges us to make that number infinite. He also tells us that in doing so we come closer to fulfilling the law than anyone who tries to do so one commandment at a time. So today, let's start worrying about the essence more and the letter less as we learn to uphold the law in the same way that Jesus does.

~

"But the gateway to life is very narrow and the road is difficult, and only a few ever find it." —Matthew 7:14 (NLT)

Read Matthew 7:13, 14

Why is it that so few find the narrow gate? Why is it that the highway to Hell is so choked with traffic while the path to Heaven often shows little signs of use? Because the message of Satan rings true with the sinful desires in people. Pride, greed, and narcissism, are in direct conflict with humility, self-denial, and reliance on a Savior. The message of the world is "anything you want, you had better grab for yourself" while the message of Christ is "Rest in Me." Satan is still in charge of this world, for the moment, and he has designed everything in this world to turn people away from God. If possible, even those who are following Jesus. Satan wants to lead everyone down the superhighway, full of billboards and flashing neon lights, straight to destruction. I pray we are all determined to find and enter the narrow gate. Not by sheer will or brute force, but by abiding in the One who stands at the gate ready to open it for anyone willing to enter.

~

"Yes, just as you can identify a tree by its fruit, so you can identify people by their actions." —Matthew 7:20 (NLT)

Read Matthew 7:15-20

The people who can do the most harm to you are the ones you cannot recognize. They sound good and may even look good, but they leave behind a trail of hurt and destruction. Sometimes they may not even recognize themselves for what they are. But Jesus said if we are watchful, we will be able to identify them by their actions. So how do we know what actions to look for? Well, some are intuitive and some we will know only if we read and understand God's Word. Some people will even take pieces of scripture and use them to their advantage, so it is important that we each know the Bible through our own study. That way we can, as Paul says, rightly divide truth from error and know the difference between fruits of the Spirit and fruits of wickedness. May we all continue to bury God's Word deep in our hearts so that fruit from the wrong trees does not poison our relationship with the Heavenly Father.

~

"Not everyone who calls out to me, 'Lord! Lord!' will enter the Kingdom of Heaven." —Matthew 7:21 (NLT)

Read Matthew 7:21-23

In our lifetimes, we will be able to fool a lot of people. There will be times when we will tell people one thing, but think another. There will be times that we put on a good face even when we have a bad heart. But, even when we have hidden our actions and feelings from everyone else, there is still One who knows the truth. We can pretend to love and follow Him in public, but He knows what we really do and what is really in our heart. On the day that we stand before Him, we will not be able to fool anyone. Let's use the mirror of scripture to get a good look at how the Father sees us, and worry less about how we look to others. And, let's work on our relationship with Him, so that He is able to recognize us when we reunite at His Son's return.

~

"Anyone who listens to my teaching and follows it is wise, like a person who builds a house on solid rock." –Matthew 7:24 (NLT)

Read Matthew 7:24-27

What is the price of ignoring the teachings of Jesus? It is the inability to stand when life opens up on us. But when we have faith in Jesus and obey His teachings, we can take whatever life throws at us because our foundation is secure. When we give up the sand for the solid rock of a foundation in Christ, we can rest. Why? Because we know that our faith is anchored to the Cross, and Christ's sacrifice for us on the cross is an act that cannot be undone. Not by the strongest wind or wave.

~

When Jesus had finished saying these things, the crowds were amazed at his teaching, for he taught with real authority—quite unlike their teachers of religious law. - Matthew 7:28, 29 NLT

Unlike other teachers of His day, Jesus did not simply recite scripture or law to the people. He told them, and us, the real meaning of the words and how to obey them in practical ways. He taught what it really meant to be a faithful citizen in God's Holy Kingdom. And He did it in a way that left no doubt that He was the author of the message and not just the messenger. Even today, His message rings true because He taught in a way that addresses the human condition regardless of the age we live in. I pray that we take His teachings to heart, for He gave them to us so that we would understand the wonderful reward that awaits those who follow Him through this life and into eternity.

~ 8 ~

"Don't tell anyone about this. Instead, go to the priest and let him examine you." –Matthew 8:4 (NLT)

Read Matthew 8:1-4

Why would Jesus not want this man to tell anyone what had happened? Because in those days a person who had the disease of leprosy, did not declare themselves healed. If the man had done that, no one would have believed him. Imagine telling someone that you had cancer and that you were miraculously healed; but you never went to a doctor so he or she could verify it. By law, the man with leprosy had to be examined by the priest who would then declare him well. Once given a clean bill of health, the man would have a good testimony about how Jesus had healed him. The same is true for us today. In our rush to give a testimony about what Christ has done for us, we sometimes are tempted to cut corners or embellish our stories. But Jesus wants honest testimonies about real interactions. We do not have to be in a hurry or change the details of our encounters with Christ. People do not believe because of what we say. They believe because of the power of the Holy Spirit working in their lives. They listen because something about our lives strikes a chord with their own life. The point is not whether our testimony is miraculous. In fact, stretching the truth actually sabotages our testimony. I pray that when we tell others about Jesus, we talk about things that have actually happened to us that can be verified. When we share personal, verifiable events from our lives, our testimony can be trusted and we can lean on God for the results.

~

"Lord, I am not worthy to have you come into my home. Just say the word from where you are, and my servant will be healed." –Matthew 8:8 (NLT)

Read Matthew 8:5-13

True humility is not about bowing and scraping or beating ourselves up all the time. It is about understanding that we all have a duty as servants. It is about understanding that in this life we all have people that answer to us and that we answer to. And it is about understanding that, ultimately, our Father in heaven is who we serve, even when we are serving others. The Roman officer knew that, even though many of the Jews in that day did not understand. Jesus commended the soldier for his faith because true faith cannot happen in the absence of true humility. So what about us? Is humility walking hand in hand with faith in our lives? I pray that we understand, just as the Roman officer did, that nothing works as it should until we understand our true station in life.

~

This fulfilled the word of the Lord through the prophet Isaiah, who said, "He took our sicknesses and removed our diseases." —Matthew 8:17

(NLT)

Read Matthew 8:14-17

Once again, Matthew takes the opportunity to remind the Jewish readers, for whom this gospel was written, that everything Jesus did had been predicted centuries before His arrival. There are hundreds of prophesies in the Old Testament that were fulfilled in the person of Jesus Christ. Many more prophesies were made about His return. If any book, other than the bible, made ten predictions that came true, people would be buying every copy on the shelf and searching out the author for more answers. Yet, even Christians sometimes have a blasé attitude about the Bible. Let's be intentional to treat God's Word with the reverence it deserves and heed not only prophesies that were fulfilled, but also those that are yet to be.

~

"Teacher, I will follow you wherever you go." But Jesus replied, "Foxes have dens to live in, and birds have nests, but the Son of Man has no place even to lay his head." —Matthew 8:19-20 (NLT)

Read Matthew 8:18-22

Following Jesus is not without cost. At some point all of us have to choose between Jesus and possessions, or Jesus and status, or Jesus and relationships. But in reality, all of these situations are really a choice between Jesus and ourselves. Are we willing to give up things that comfort us? Are we willing to give up things that build up our pride? Are we willing to give up our friends? The real question is not WHAT are we willing to give up but rather what are WE willing to give up. If we are willing, Jesus stands ready to walk with us and teach us about ourselves through the choices we make. We may go a long time without being confronted by such a decision. But when we are, I pray that we make the wise one.

~

The disciples were amazed. "Who is this man?" they asked. "Even the winds and waves obey him!" –Matthew 8:27 (NLT)

Read Matthew 8:23-27

The bottom line is this: Everything must obey God in the end. Storms are going to attack us while we live on this earth because, like us, the earth has been corrupted by sin. But faith in the One who has dominion over everything will see us through the storms of this life. Does that mean that every storm will be quelled? No. But, it does mean that in every storm, Christ walks with us and guides us to teach us more about ourselves and more about Him. Through Paul, God promised that He will not take us through more than He knows we can handle and, if we face the storm in faith, He will change us along the way. Whatever storm we may be facing, let's face it in faith and trust the Father to make us a better person through it.

~

"All right, go!" Jesus commanded them. So the demons came out of the men and entered the pigs, and the whole herd plunged down the steep hillside into the lake and drowned in the water. —Matthew 8:32 (NLT)

Read Matthew 8:28-34

What demons do you face today? We all have them. Each of us has fears, desires, anxieties, or passions. If we do not fight them every day, the demons in our lives will lead us down the highway of sin. But even the demons have no choice but to obey God. If we continue to abide in His Son, then He will take those burdens away, in His time. As long as we rest in Him, the demons can only do what He allows, so go to Him today and ask for His forgiveness, His grace, and His protection. When we do, we have the peace that comes from knowing that the One who controls the universe is in control of our situation as well.

~

"Then the entire town came out to meet Jesus, but they begged him to go away and leave them alone." –Matthew 8:34 (NLT)

Read Matthew 8:28-34 (Again)

There is a second lesson in this passage. There are going to be times when, even in the face of overwhelming evidence for the sovereignty of Jesus, people are going to reject Him. It's not that they do not understand what they have seen or heard. It's not even a matter of whether or not they believe who He is. Some people will just refuse to allow Him into their lives. Whether it is fear about what they might have to give up, or pride that says they are too smart to believe, or any other reason, they will simply reject Him. I pray that when others reject Jesus, we remember that it is not something new and just as He continued to preach the gospel, so should we continue to tell others about Him. What others do with that information is between them and God.

~ 9 ~

Seeing their faith, Jesus said to the paralyzed man, "Be encouraged, my child! Your sins are forgiven." But some of the teachers of religious law said to themselves, "That's blasphemy! Does he think he's God —Matthew 9:2, 3 NLT

Read Matthew 9:1-8

Jesus knew that this man's spiritual well-being was far more important than his physical one. You see, we all face problems in this life. When we least expect them, medical issues, financial problems, emotional trouble, and relationship matters, all seem to jump out and cripple us. But even though we can see them and experience them in tangible ways, these problems are small compared to the one we cannot see, feel, or hear. We are completely lost in sin with no hope of ever being able to navigate our way out. No matter what we do, we will never be perfect, and perfect is exactly what is required to leave destruction behind and enter into eternity. Jesus knew it, and the Pharisees knew it as well. The Pharisees knew that their brand of redemption was symbolic at best and they were threatened by the message of true grace being taught by the Carpenter, so they challenged Him. The result was Jesus using the man's paralysis to demonstrate what the response to forgiveness should be. Through faith, the man believed he would be healed. So, when healed by Jesus, he got up, picked up his mat, and left. Through faith we should believe that our sins have been forgiven, leave behind the trappings that accompany our sin, and begin our new life in Christ. The only question is, "Will we?"

~

But when the Pharisees saw this, they asked his disciples, "Why does your teacher eat with such scum?" When Jesus heard this, he said, "Healthy people don't need a doctor—sick people do." —Matthew 9:11, 12 (NLT)

Read Matthew 9:9-13

Do you know that you are a sinner? Not in some general sense but in a personal way that leaves you with the knowledge that, on your own, you are not going to make it? There is good news. You are the reason Jesus came to earth and sacrificed Himself. You are the one that He came to save. You are the one that He came to redeem. He came for you, and me, and everyone else. I pray that we never lose the reality that on our own we are lost. Because the only person who cannot be made well is the one who is convinced that he is not sick.

~

"And no one puts new wine into old wineskins. For the old skins would burst from the pressure, spilling the wine and ruining the skins. New wine is stored in new wineskins so that both are preserved." —Matthew 9:17 *(NLT)*

Read Matthew 9:14-17

Who knows the law better, the person who reads it or the person who wrote it? The religious leaders had been studying and following the law for hundreds of years. But during that time, they had made changes to the law. They trying to refine it to the point that no one could say they did not know what was required of them. The problem with their effort was that the religious leaders had left the intent of the law behind. Jesus, the author of the law, came to teach us its true meaning, how it would be fulfilled, and why it was important. What He was teaching could not fit in as part of the old doctrine. In order to follow Him, people would have to leave the old cloth, the old wineskin, and the old teaching behind. People would have to be willing to be filled by the new wine that was the perfect interpretation of the original law by the actual writer. The same is true for us. There are teachers who would have us memorize lists of commandments and laws so that we can follow all of them. Jesus said the list is only two items long. People today would tell us that following the teaching of the law means learning to be perfect. Jesus tells us that we cannot be. There are those who tell us when we are not perfect that we can fix our imperfection by sacrificing something or offering prayers. Jesus says there is only one sacrifice we can trust in to erase our sins. Let's follow the Author and trust Him for the true interpretation of the law. For His only interest is getting us home…in new clothing.

~

Just then a woman who had suffered for twelve years with constant bleeding came up behind him. She touched the fringe of his robe, for she thought, "If I can just touch his robe, I will be healed." —Matthew 9:20, 21 (NLT)

Read Matthew 9:18-22

How long do we struggle with a problem before we take it to Christ? I know I have a particular problem with doing everything I can to fix things on my own, and THEN, if nothing works, I think to take it to Him. The woman in this story had the same strategy. Another gospel says that she tried several doctors and other remedies during her twelve years of suffering. Why do we do that? Why do we wait so long before asking the One who has the power over everything? In a word, pride. We are so sure we can handle our struggles on our own that we do not even think about asking Jesus for help. But, asking in faith is always the best thing we can do. If we ask first, then we can be sure that Jesus will move heaven and earth to give us the best solution to whatever problem we bring to Him. When the woman asked, Jesus stopped what He was doing to take care of her. When we find ourselves in the valley, we should take time to touch the hem of Jesus' garment as well, and watch Him turn to us in our time of need.

~

When Jesus arrived at the official's home, he saw the noisy crowd and heard the funeral music. "Get out!" he told them. "The girl isn't dead; she's only asleep" —Matthew 9:23, 24 (NLT)

Read Matthew 9:23-26

Can you imagine what was going through the official's mind when he got home and found that his daughter had died? If they had not been delayed by the woman who grabbed Jesus' robe then maybe they would have gotten home while she was still sick and Jesus could have healed her. Now, was it too late? He could heal the sick, but could even Jesus bring someone back from the dead? Would you have been mad at the woman? Would you have been mad at Jesus for stopping? Would you have thought that all hope was lost? The official did the same thing the woman with the issue did. He asked. But Jesus did not take care of his problem...or so he thought. Our problem is we always think we know the best way to fix a problem. But God tells us that His thoughts are so much higher than our thoughts and His ways are so much better than our ways. Depending on the girl's illness, people could have said she got well on her own and Jesus had nothing to do with her healing. But no one recovers from death. No one comes back on their own once their heart stops beating and their brain ceases to function. No one could dispute that Jesus had raised her from the dead. The number of people who believed in God because of that act was exponential compared to who would have believed a child's illness being cured. Because Jesus did it His way, the girl was healed and the multitudes believed. What are you waiting for Jesus to do in your life? Does it appear that help is not coming? Does it seem that hope is lost? Do you think that you have been forgotten or ignored? I pray today that you look up in faith. The night is always darkest just before the dawn and Jesus is bringing the light. Trust in Him and He will see you through your struggle.

~

After Jesus left the girl's home, two blind men followed along behind him, shouting, "Son of David, have mercy on us!" –Matthew 9:27 (NLT)

Read Matthew 9:27-31

In the last few sections, we have seen people with problems ask, we have seen people with problems believe, and we have seen people with problems receive answers. But there is one other characteristic they all shared and we need to make sure we see it. They were bold! They had heard what this Carpenter from Nazareth could do. They knew they needed help no one else could give them. And they were not going to be denied! They did not hang back and hope to be noticed. They did not write a letter. No, they approached Him confidently, they grabbed His clothes, and they followed Him all the way into His own house because they were determined to at least get an audience with Christ. They did not know if they would receive what they asked, but they knew they were going to ask. Let's be the same way. Let's go to the throne boldly; knowing that in Christ there is no disappointment. My prayer, in boldness, is that we demonstrate our faith by asking our Lord, in confidence, for the needs of the day.

~

The crowds were amazed. "Nothing like this has ever happened in Israel!" they exclaimed. But the Pharisees said, "He can cast out demons because he is empowered by the prince of demons." - Matthew 9:33-34 NLT

Read Matthew 9:32-34

It is safe to say that Jesus was not a crowd favorite among the Pharisees. When they could not refute what Jesus was doing, the Pharisees tried to explain it away as power received from Satan. Of course even that tactic does not hold water. But, it is a good example of how the world will stop at nothing, including vilifying those who profess the gospel of grace found in Jesus Christ. Jesus warned His followers they could expect no better than He received from the world. So let's remember that when the world calls us antiquated, when the world calls us bigots, when the world calls us intolerant, they are doing so out of the same desperation that led the Pharisees to call Jesus demonic. Remember, even then, He did not hate. Instead, He continued to spread His message, and He calls us to do the same today.

~

When he saw the crowds, he had compassion on them because they were confused and helpless, like sheep without a shepherd. —Matthew 9:36 (NLT)

Read Matthew 9:35-38

Over seven billion people inhabit this spinning rock. Do you know that it is God's desire that all would be saved? Everywhere Jesus went, He had compassion for people, not because they were already followers but because they were not. People were confused and helpless. They were being led around by others who were headed into more sin. Even today, unholy shepherds look to lead people deeper into greed, pride, and sexual sin by telling them they deserve it, they need it, and they want it. Should our desire not be the same as God's? Should we not want more and more people to come into a saving relationship with Christ? But how can they have that relationship without knowing Him? How can they know Him without hearing about Him? How will they hear about Him if no one is there to tell them? As long as there is one person left on earth who does not know about Christ, there is a need for someone to tell them. So let's pray today that God would inspire more people to move on to the next step in their Christian walk and begin to tell others the Good News. The work is not done until everyone has been told and the need for workers will continue until that day, when everyone has heard, and the Son returns.

~ 10 ~

"Go and announce to them that the Kingdom of Heaven is near. Heal the sick, raise the dead, cure those with leprosy, and cast out demons. Give as freely as you have received!" —Matthew 10:7, 8 (NLT)

Read Matthew 10:1-8

How freely have we received? Someone we did not know, many years before we were born, gave His own life so we might have forgiveness, even from sins we have not yet committed. And what have we done to deserve the gift of forgiveness? Absolutely nothing. And, knowing what we have received, we are still uncomfortable mentioning Jesus' name around others. But we have been called, just as Peter and John and the rest were called; not only to proclaim His name, but testify to what He did for us on the cross as well. I pray today that when we have the opportunity to witness, we give as freely as we have received.

~

"If any household or town refuses to welcome you or listen to your message, shake its dust from your feet as you leave. I tell you the truth, the wicked cities of Sodom and Gomorrah will be better off than such a town on the judgment day." —Matthew 10:14, 15 (NLT)

Read Matthew 10:9-15

We are all called to spread the gospel of Jesus Christ. No matter where we are or who we are with, we should look for opportunities to tell others about the grace available to us through Him. If those we are talking to refuse that message, then that decision is on them. They will answer for it when their life here is done. Our responsibility is simply to share the message by telling others about Jesus and showing His love by our actions. So, as opportunities arise, we should fulfill our Christian duty, to spread the message, of the eternal life we receive when we trust in the Savior and rest in His work on the cross.

~

"You will stand trial before governors and kings because you are my followers. But this will be your opportunity to tell the rulers and other unbelievers about me." —Matthew 10:18 (NLT)

Read Matthew 10:16-20

Have be you ever been challenged for being a Christian? Have you ever been harassed at work or school because you show your faith? Consider yourself privileged because you are there for a reason! Some people will never willingly sit and listen to the gospel, but we will have our chance, when we are being persecuted, to both speak and show this hope that lives within us. Notice that Jesus did not say if we are persecuted, but when we are persecuted. We will all face persecution or be challenged at some point in our lives. My prayer for those whose time is today is that they will listen to the Holy Spirit. If they do then the Father will give them the words to say and perhaps another soul will enter into eternity.

~

"But everyone who endures to the end will be saved." —Matthew 10:22 (NLT)

Read Matthew 10:21, 22

What will you have to give up for following Christ? Did you know that, even today, there are Christians who suffer at the hands of their own families for sitting at the feet of Jesus? We have chosen to follow the One who is diametrically opposed to the world and for that the world will hate us. But my prayer this morning is that, no matter the level of persecution we have to face, we endure to the end. For the reward for those who finish is beyond measure and the punishment for those who do not will be the same as that which awaits the world they chose to follow.

~

"And since I, the master of the household, have been called the prince of demons, the members of my household will be called by even worse names!"
—Matthew 10:25 (NLT)

Read Matthew 10:23-25

When we see how Jesus was treated by non-believers, should we really be surprised by the treatment we get from them today? What we need to remember in those situations where we are being treated badly is we should also respond the same way that He did. Responding to others the same way Jesus did is really the hard part. Our prayer should be that we feel the strength available through the Holy Spirit to react properly to the way we are treated. In all our dealings with non-believers, we need to remember the purpose of all this is to get the message of Christ to the non-believer; even if they are persecuting us for doing so. Remember, just as we must suffer the same things as the Teacher, we will also reap the same rewards...life everlasting and a personal relationship with the Creator of the universe.

~

"Everyone who acknowledges me publicly here on earth, I will also acknowledge before my Father in heaven. But everyone who denies me here on earth, I will also deny before my Father in heaven." —Matthew 10:32, 33 (NLT)

Read Matthew 10:28-33

The fears that keep us from talking about Jesus can be diverse. Fear of people, fear of persecution, fear of rejection, fear of embarrassment, fear of being labeled. There are any number of phobias that keep us from proclaiming our faith. It is strange, when you think about it; that we fear such things, but we do not fear the wrath of God. What can people do to us compared to the One who sees everything and knows us so well that He even knows how many hairs we have on our head? We fear someone who seems to hold our job in their hands, but do we fear the One who holds our eternity? He is the One who judges and He does it solely on the testimony of His Son. His Son makes it very clear, acknowledge Me and I will acknowledge you. Equally clear is the message, deny Me and I will deny you. It really boils down to this...What should we fear more, temporary inconveniences or permanent rejection? The latter is as real an option as the former, and believing in our hearts is not enough. Confessing with our mouths is also required regardless of what it might cost us now.

~

"If you cling to your life, you will lose it; but if you give up your life for me, you will find it." —Matthew 10:39 (NLT)

Read Matthew 10:34-39

We, as followers of Christ will be forced to make decisions. Friends, acquaintances, and yes, even family members will turn away from us, unless we give up sitting at the feet of the Master. The temptation will be to remain silent about our faith around such people in an attempt to maintain the relationship. But Jesus Himself warns us that that behavior is not acceptable. Even when it comes to our family, Jesus must be first or our faith is pointless. When He is first, we receive not only the object of our faith, but also a new and improved life. It is a difficult decision when we look at things through temporal lenses. But through the eyes of faith, we can see the eternal reward. And we are able to trust in the plan that God has for both us and the ones we leave behind. I pray we keep the eternal view in mind. Only then are we are able to make the decision that leads to life, for everyone.

~

"Anyone who receives you receives me, and anyone who receives me receives the Father who sent me." -Matthew 10:40 (NLT)

Read Matthew 10:40-42

Jesus makes it clear that aiding those who work in His name brings its own reward. Not everyone is gifted to speaking about the gospel, but everyone can help spread the gospel, even if it is by helping someone who does speak. In whatever way we are gifted to aid in the advancement of God's word, we should do so in the power of the Holy Spirit. Even if it is simply to quench someone's thirst.

~ 11 ~

John the Baptist, who was in prison, heard about all the things the Messiah was doing. So he sent his disciples to ask Jesus, "Are you the Messiah we've been expecting, or should we keep looking for someone else?" –
Matthew 11:2-3 (NLT)

Read Matthew 11:1-6

No matter who we are or how strong our faith is, there will be times of doubt in our lives. John the Baptist spent his entire life announcing the coming Messiah. He was even given the privilege of presenting Jesus to the world on the day of Jesus' baptism. But even after all his work, as John spent his last days in prison, he had doubts. Yes, doubt will come to all of us at some point. The question is not will we have doubt, but rather what will we do when doubt comes? Will we allow it to lead us off in the wrong direction? Or will we, like John, bring our questions to Jesus so He can reassure us and strengthen us so we can face our struggles? My prayer this morning is that we take John's path back to Jesus so that we will receive the blessing promised to those who do not allow doubt to cause us to take the wrong turn.

~

"I tell you the truth, of all who have ever lived, none is greater than John the Baptist. Yet even the least person in the Kingdom of Heaven is greater than he is!" –Matthew 11:7-11 (NLT)

Read Matthew 11:7-15

Do not miss the importance of John the Baptist's ministry. John the Baptist was the herald of history, the announcer of the Messiah, and the one whose ministry proclaimed the end of the old ways and the beginning of the new. And yet, according to Jesus, John's importance is dwarfed by the least of those who believe in Him. Do not miss our importance, not because of who we are but because of what we hold. We have the gospel of grace found in Jesus Christ. Just as it was important for John to announce Jesus' coming, it is more important for us to announce that He has been here, He has saved us, and He is coming back. John's message was do not miss the opportunity when He gets here. Our message is do not miss the opportunity NOW, because tomorrow is promised to no one. When the Son of God comes this time it will be to collect those who believed in Him. And on that day, the opportunity to accept Jesus will have passed. I pray we understand who we are, whose we are, and the importance of what we carry. Let's not clutch the good news of Jesus tightly to our chest. Rather let's display that news for all to see, so that more and more may have the opportunity to believe while it is still today.

~

'We played wedding songs, and you didn't dance, so we played funeral songs, and you didn't mourn.' —*Matthew 11:17 (NLT)*

Read Matthew 11:16-19

There are always going to be people who simply will not believe. No matter how the gospel is presented, some people will always have an excuse for not following Jesus. To them, Christians will, at times, be religious nuts for following Christ or hypocrites for not following the Law. But in the end, these are all excuses to relieve themselves of their responsibility to face the truth. But that should not be an excuse for us to withhold the truth from them. We will all answer for our actions concerning the gospel one day. Did we accept it? Did we present it? Did we live it? Let's fulfill our responsibilities now so that on that day we will not be the ones who are left with excuses.

~

"For if the miracles I did for you had been done in wicked Sodom, it would still be here today. I tell you, even Sodom will be better off on judgment day than you." —Matthew 11:23, 24 (NLT)

Read Matthew 11:20-24

Those towns made famous in the Old Testament were known for their utter wickedness. If there was anything contrary to God's law, it was practiced in these cities. But the people of those towns had never heard about Jesus, never heard the gospel, and never had the opportunity to believe. Those of us who have lived since Jesus cannot say the same thing. Especially today, and in this country, you would be hard pressed to find someone who has heard nothing about Jesus. And, for all those who have heard of Him, there is a decision to make. The consequence of that decision, though seemingly small now, can be life changing or life ending. So we must make a choice. I pray we choose wisely. For the one argument we will not be allowed when we stand before the throne is the excuse of not knowing.

~

"For my yoke is easy to bear, and the burden I give you is light." –
Matthew 11:30 (NLT)

Read Matthew 11:25-30

The people of Jesus' day toiled under the requirements put upon them by the religious leaders. They required the people to live perfectly under the law and addendum even when they did not. Even today, people who do not know Christ labor under their own convictions, or the convictions placed upon them by others that define what kind of person they should be. The people in Jesus' time refused Him out of fear that they would be exchanging one yoke for another that was heavier. But the truth is those who choose to follow Christ find their life is not filled with crushing and impossible to follow rules. Instead, those who follow Him enter into a partnership with the Holy Spirit. In that partnership, the Spirit comes alongside to guide us as we fulfill the true spirit of the Law; loving God and loving others. The Holy Spirit also consoles us and encourages us as we walk through troubles here on earth. But most importantly, our acceptance of Christ means we have placed our mistakes and our sins beneath the blood of the perfect sacrifice. We never have to worry about whether we have done enough to cover our sins by ourselves. My prayer today is that more people would discover just how light the burden of knowing and following Christ truly is, and that they accept the rest that He offers to all.

~ 12 ~

"For the Son of Man is Lord, even over the Sabbath!" - *Matthew 12:1-8*
NLT

Read Matthew 12:1-8

For many of the laws that God handed down to Moses, the Pharisees had created numerous rules for whether or not that law had been violated. One of the most glaring examples were rules regarding rest on the Sabbath. Walking one-half of a mile on the Sabbath was ok, but walking three quarters of a mile was work. Assisting someone who was in need was work. Even picking a head of grain and eating it was considered work. The Pharisees knew that the Israeli nation had spent seventy years in exile for disobeying God, so they spent the next four hundred years trying to make sure that no one broke another law, even accidentally. But, they had missed the boat entirely. God was not interested in how well they followed the rules. He wanted them to get the point of the rules. He loved them and He wanted their love in return. If you love someone, you do things that please them. If you love someone, you love those they love. Israel did not go into exile for breaking the rules. They were exiled because they no longer had a heart for God. What about us? Do we have a heart for God? If we do, then our heart guides us into doing what is right. When we do not have a heart for God, we will not be able to follow the rules, even if we try. So let's examine our hearts in the light of scripture and see where they lay. Do we worry more about obeying the letter of every rule, or about the mercy of helping those who are in need? When we choose the latter, we have a heart that is chasing God and the spirit of the law is fulfilled.

~

The Pharisees asked Jesus, "Does the law permit a person to work by healing on the Sabbath?" —Matthew 12:10 (NLT)

Read Matthew 12:9-14

How often do we use God as an excuse? That is what the Pharisees were doing. They were using their pretense of following God's Law to condemn one innocent man to a continued handicap and another to death. When we use the Law in a way that prevents us from helping others, then we are just as hypocritical as the Pharisees were. All of the Law given to us by God should point us to loving Him and loving others. When the Law points us away from those things then it is being wielded improperly. During those times, we need to look inward to determine what is driving our actions. The Pharisees improperly applied the Law because they were motivated by pride and jealously. What motivates us? The good news is that if we recognize what motivates us, we can change it, if necessary. And if we can change our hearts we can learn to use God's Law the way it was intended.

~

"He will not fight or shout or raise his voice in public. He will not crush the weakest reed or put out a flickering candle." —Matthew 12:19, 20 NLT

Read Matthew 12:15-21

Jesus did not, and does not, force Himself on others. His teaching has stood the test of time, not because of its forcefulness, but because of its quiet truth. Even those who do not believe in Jesus cannot argue with what He taught. Even His declaration that He was the only way to God was a quiet statement of fact and not a shouted proclamation of self-promotion. So let's tell those, who push Him away for fear that He will force Himself on them, to take courage. Jesus stands at the door and knocks, but He does not break in and He will not force Himself into your heart. Jesus quietly presents the truth and leaves the decision to you. If He didn't, the decision would be meaningless.

~

But when the Pharisees heard about the miracle, they said, "No wonder he can cast out demons. He gets his power from Satan, the prince of demons."
—Matthew 12:24 (NLT)

Read Matthew 12:22-29

The Pharisees were desperate to discredit Jesus. But their arguments and accusations never held up. The same is true today. There will always be those who have arguments and excuses for not believing in Christ. But just like those of the Pharisees, their arguments cannot stand against God's word. Take time to study the scriptures rather than listening to the hollow arguments of men. As we grow in God's truth, the Holy Spirit will be able to use us to put all arguments to flight and those who produce them will be left with the naked reality that they simply refuse to believe, without a good reason.

~

"Anyone who speaks against the Son of Man can be forgiven, but anyone who speaks against the Holy Spirit will never be forgiven, either in this world or in the world to come." —Matthew 12:32 (NLT)

Read Matthew 12:30-32

Jesus does not give us many choices when it comes to believing in Him. Either we are with Him or we are against Him. Not only are we against Him, but, as He says, we are actively working against Him. How? When we refuse to believe, we speak against what the Holy Spirit is doing in our lives and in the lives of others. It may be subtle, subtle even to the point that we do not see it, but we are always working against Him to defend our choice to not believe. That is why actively working against the Holy Spirit is the only sin that cannot be forgiven. We can only be forgiven of our sins if we accept Christ as our Savior; but we cannot accept Him as savior as long as we are speaking against the Holy Spirit. If we insist upon speaking against the Holy Spirit throughout this life, then forgiveness will never be available to us and we are truly lost. My prayer is that those who have chosen to work against Christ and speak against the Holy

Spirit would come to understand the gravity of their decision before the opportunity is no longer available. Tomorrow is promised to no one and today will be over before we know it.

~

"And I tell you this, you must give an account on judgment day for every idle word you speak. The words you say will either acquit you or condemn you."
—Matthew 12:36, 37 (NLT)

Read Matthew 12:33-37

Want to know what is in someone's heart? Just listen to what they have to say. Sure, someone with a bad heart may be able to sweeten their speech for short periods of time, but if you spend enough time around them, they will betray their true feelings. The real test is what we say when we are not "on guard". The idle words we will be judged by are the ones we speak when we feel comfortable enough to talk without our filter. Those words reveal the true condition of our hearts and we should pay attention to them. When we find ourselves speaking words that produce bad fruit, let's pray we recognize it for the warning sign that it is and go to the Lord for help. For only He can help us remove the evil from our hearts.

~

One day some teachers of religious law and Pharisees came to Jesus and said, "Teacher, we want you to show us a miraculous sign to prove your authority." -Matthew 12:38 (NLT)

Read Matthew 12:38-45

There will be times when we are talking to others about Christ, that they will try to excuse their unbelief by saying that they have never seen anything miraculous or that they were expecting a miracle that never happened. But the truth is, the only miracle that really matters is the one that happened at the death and resurrection of Jesus. Because of that miracle we have a path to forgiveness and everlasting life. All other miracles are pointless if we do not believe and accept the miracle of Jesus' death and resurrection. Those who demand proof before believing already have all they need. The demand itself is just an excuse to not believe. People who hear and understand what they are being told, but refuse to believe are even worse off than those who have never heard, because they are now without excuse. So let's pray that those we speak to understand and accept what was done for them through Christ's miraculous sacrifice. Though other miracles may appear in our lives, it is the only one that truly matters.

~

"Anyone who does the will of my Father in heaven is my brother and sister and mother!" —Matthew 12:50 (NLT)

Read Matthew 12:46-50

Jesus made it very plain: entrance to the heavenly family is dependent upon one thing; doing the will of the Father. What is that? What is the will of the Father? It is simply accepting what He has already done for us through His Son. When we take that step, we become a son or daughter. We become heirs to the kingdom and brothers and sisters to all who have done likewise. Our earthly family was given to us at our first birth. Our heavenly one is received at our second. Our prayer should always be that every day the family of Christ multiplies. The more who join God's family, the fewer left behind to face the wrath to come. And just imagine what the reunion will be like!

~ 13 ~

"But blessed are your eyes, because they see; and your ears, because they hear. I tell you the truth, many prophets and righteous people longed to see what you see, but they didn't see it. And they longed to hear what you hear, but they didn't hear it. —Matthew 13:16, 17 (NLT)

Read Matthew 13:1-17

Parables can be as confusing today for those who read them as they were for those who first heard them. Jesus' point is this; those who are willing to read the parables, seeking to understand them, will comprehend them. But those who do not read or look at the parables with a real desire to know will never understand their true meaning. It is a message to us about how we should approach our study of scripture. Do we read God's word with a spirit of reverence and a desire to learn? Or do we read as if performing a duty or penance, not really searching for understanding of what we read? If it is the former, our eyes will see, our ears will hear, and our hearts will understand. If it is the latter, we are in the dark, and not even looking for the light switch.

~

"The seed that fell on good soil represents those who truly hear and understand God's word and produce a harvest of thirty, sixty, or even a hundred times as much as had been planted!" —Matthew 13:23 (NLT)

Read Matthew 13:18-23

There are many hurdles in spreading the gospel of Jesus Christ. There are those who just refuse to listen. Then, there are those who hear and believe, but turn away because their faith is not deep or they are lured away by other things in this world. However, some people will hear and believe. Because of their belief, the gospel will continue to spread. Notice the parable does not say the farmer gave up and went home because of the failed plants. Let's keep that in mind as we work in communion with the Holy Spirit to spread the message of Christ. When we are tempted to give up because we are scattering seed in barren places, let's remember that God is in control and fertile soil can be found in the driest of places.

~

"'Should we pull out the weeds?' they asked. "' No,' he replied, 'you'll uproot the wheat if you do. Let both grow together until the harvest. Then I will tell the harvesters to sort out the weeds, tie them into bundles, and burn them, and to put the wheat in the barn.'" –Matthew 13:28-30 (NLT)

Read Matthew 13:24-30

Would it not be great if the only people around us were other believers? We would not have to worry about what we would see or hear. We would not be tempted to do the things that non-believers do, because we would not be living next to them, watching them appear to get away with sin. We would not have to choose between good and bad, right and wrong, or others and self. But that is not God's plan and all I can say is thank goodness. You see, when we are tempted to look down at the weeds around us we only need to remember one thing. We all started out as weeds! Thankfully, God has the wisdom to wait until the harvest to remove the weeds. Just think about where we would be if He had removed us while we were still weeds, before someone talked to us about Christ, before we had given our hearts to the Lord, before we had the chance to change from weeds to wheat. What's more, we did not become wheat by hanging around other weeds. No, we learned our faith by hanging around wheat. Now, it is our turn to be wheat to other weeds. So instead of wishing we did not have to hang out among the weeds, let's be diligent in spreading the gospel to all of those weeds around us. If we do, the next time we look around, we may just see more heads of wheat and less fuel for the fire.

~

Jesus always used stories and illustrations like these when speaking to the crowds. In fact, he never spoke to them without using such parables. This fulfilled what God had spoken through the prophet: "I will speak to you in parables. I will explain things hidden since the creation of the world." –
Matthew 13:34, 35 (NLT)

Read Matthew 13:31-35

Dozens of times, Matthew points out how Old Testament prophecy is fulfilled in the person and action of Jesus Christ. Matthew was trying to show the Jewish nation with his gospel that Jesus was indeed the Messiah they had been waiting for. But just as they were unable to understand Christ's parables, preconceived ideas about what their Savior would be like kept the Jewish nation from believing this simple, humble teacher was in fact the Son of God. That danger is just as real for us today. It is easy for us to decide whether or not Jesus is real by what He does, or does not do, for us. It is important for us to remember that Jesus has already done everything we need, and more than we deserve, by taking the punishment for our sin. What happens to us as we live our daily lives is inconsequential to who

Jesus is as our Savior. I pray that instead of believing the lie that says, "if God cared He would not allow us to suffer", we look to the truth of scripture that says Christ has already done what is necessary to protect us for eternity.

~

"Just as the weeds are sorted out and burned in the fire, so it will be at the end of the world." —Matthew 13:40 (NLT)

Read Matthew 13:36-43

Forces in this world are constantly at work to keep us from thinking about the future and the consequences of our actions. But Jesus tells us that as much as we would like to live in the moment, a time is coming when we will all have to face the consequences of our decisions. He makes it clear what the decisions are that must be made by everyone and the consequences for each. While we should be mindful of those around us today and work to convey the message of salvation to them, let's not forget that we also need to be mindful of tomorrow as well. Hearing the word and choosing wisely is as important for us as it is for those we speak to. Despite what the world says, our eternal future depends upon it.

~

"Again, the Kingdom of Heaven is like a merchant on the lookout for choice pearls. When he discovered a pearl of great value, he sold everything he owned and bought it!" —Matthew 13:45, 46 (NLT)

Read Matthew 13:44-46

Christ tells us the Kingdom of Heaven is something so precious that people who truly understand what they have been given are willing to give anything to keep it. Which begs the question, "Do we understand what we have been given?" If so, what are we willing to forsake in order to hold on to what we have received? How precious is the Kingdom to us? Each of us should take the time to dwell on these questions in light of Christ's words. It is sometimes hard to value something we cannot see, cannot feel, or cannot experience. But even when we cannot see, we can believe what Jesus told us. That is why it is called Faith.

~

"Do you understand all these things?" "Yes," they said, "we do." Then he added, "Every teacher of religious law who becomes a disciple in the Kingdom of Heaven is like a homeowner who brings from his storeroom new gems of truth as well as old." —Matthew 13:51, 52 (NLT)

Read Matthew 13:47-52

The message about the coming judgment was an important one for Jesus as evidenced by His repeated references. He wanted to make sure people understood exactly what was at stake in their decision about whether or not to follow Him. Although it is not a pleasant scenario to consider, we must understand what it means for anyone who turns their back on Christ. We should continually examine our lives in light of that decision and its consequences. The stakes are real, and our commitment should be real as well.

~

Then Jesus told them, "A prophet is honored everywhere except in his own hometown and among his own family." And so he did only a few miracles there because of their unbelief. –Matthew 13:57, 58 (NLT)

Read Matthew 13:53-58

Jesus told us that as His followers we would suffer the same hardship and rejection that He did for the sake of the gospel. So why should we be surprised if we, like He, are rejected by those who know us (or think they know us) best. We cannot blame them. Most of them watched us grow up. They have seen us at our best... and at our worst. Some know secrets about us that we wish we could forget. But most of all, they remember who we used to be, so they doubt that who we are now is real. They may see it as a phase, an act, or even hypocrisy. Under the circumstances, it is easy to understand their reluctance to believe what faith in Christ has done for us. But knowing that our family and friends have seen us at our worst, does not give us a pass. Christ did not stop sharing the gospel and neither should we. None of us know whose heart the Father has prepared to receive the gospel. So just as we join Jesus in His rejection, let's join Him in His perseverance as well. For even fertile soil cannot produce a crop unless a seed is planted.

~ 14 ~

Then the king regretted what he had said; but because of the vow he had made in front of his guests, he issued the necessary orders. So John was beheaded in the prison, and his head was brought on a tray and given to the girl, who took it to her mother. —Matthew 14:9-11 (NLT)

Read Matthew 14:1-12

When we refuse God, we can expect confusion to reign in our lives. We can expect to make decisions that just do not make sense. We can expect to not know who Jesus is or what He is about. We can expect that the further we go down the road without God, the more bizarre our life will become and the stranger our choices will be. The life of Herod Antipas was a perfect example of this. Born into royalty, he took decadence to a whole new level. Among his choices; stealing his brother's wife, imprisoning the man who tried to warn him against it, and allowing himself to be seduced by his wife's daughter. The results? Manipulation by his wife, embarrassment in front of his court, and the murder of an innocent man. Worst of all, a mind so confused that Herod Antipas did not recognize Jesus for who He truly was. Herod Antipas stands as an example of the mind that refuses to obey God. I pray that each day we remember what Herod Antipas represents. Let's renew our commitment to the Father daily and walk with Him in all of our endeavors. The alternative is a path that soon clouds our mind to the point that we do not even realize we are lost.

As soon as Jesus heard the news, he left in a boat to a remote area to be alone. —Matthew 14:13 (NLT)

Read Matthew 14:13, 14

Think that Jesus was above emotion? This passage shows that even He sought solitude in times of grief. But even though He suffered through the same feelings we do, He never forgot His purpose here on earth. In humility, he put the needs of others ahead of His own, even in the face of personal loss. As His followers, we should be of the same mind. In a world that teaches everyone to take care of themselves first, Jesus placed others ahead of Himself, and challenged us to do the same. Will we accept that challenge? Can we show compassion for others even when our own world is upside down? I pray the answer is both yes and amen. For those who are first will be last and those who are last will be first in the eternity that awaits us all.

~

That evening the disciples came to him and said, "This is a remote place, and it's already getting late. Send the crowds away so they can go to the villages and buy food for themselves." But Jesus said, "That isn't necessary—you feed them." –Matthew 14:15, 16 (NLT)

Read Matthew 14:15-21

What are we afraid of losing? Money? Food? Time? Possessions? Do we hoard it, keeping it all for ourselves because we are afraid we will not have enough? The lesson in this scripture is that when we use what we have to help others there will always be enough. Not only enough, but more left over. Everything we have belongs to God anyway. It is only in our possession, temporarily, so we may use those gifts to serve His purposes. If we try to keep everything we have been given to ourselves we are sure to lose it long before we are through here. But when we give what we have freely in the Lord's service we are sure to have enough plus more. My prayer is that we use whatever we have to help others and spread the Gospel of Christ. Whatever we lose in the process will be replaced, or is something we did not really need anyway.

~

But Jesus spoke to them at once. "Don't be afraid," he said. "Take courage. I am here! " –Matthew 14:27 (NLT)

Read Matthew 14:22-27

What is your storm today? We can be sure of one thing, no matter what we are going through, Jesus is always with us through the person of the Holy Spirit. He is ready and able to quell any tempest we face, as long as we are ready to lean on Him. So let's take courage and face the storms that come our way. Whatever havoc they may wreak, there are two things we can be sure of; Jesus will never leave us and, if we keep our eyes on Him, we will always emerge changed for the better. I pray that even when the thunder is loudest and the waves tallest, we will lean on Jesus.

~

But when he saw the strong wind and the waves, he was terrified and began to sink. "Save me, Lord!" he shouted. Jesus immediately reached out and grabbed him. "You have so little faith," Jesus said. "Why did you doubt me?" —Matthew 14:30, 31 (NLT)

Read Matthew 14:28-33

It is so important that we keep our eyes on Jesus. When we do, we can be sure our faith will hold. But when we look away from Jesus and focus on the circumstances of our lives, our doubts and fears start to creep in and we soon begin to sink as our foundation erodes from under our feet. You see, where we keep our focus is really what determines our foundation. So as we go about our lives let's keep our focus on Christ, especially during the storms. When we do, He will bring us through the storm to the other shore, safe, whole, and stronger in our faith.

When the people recognized Jesus, the news of his arrival spread quickly throughout the whole area, and soon people were bringing all their sick to be healed. —Matthew 14:35 (NLT)

Read Matthew 14:34-36

Just the mention of Jesus' name brought people to Him when they were in need. People knew their needs and recognized Him as someone who could fulfill those needs. But the needs they were looking to satisfy were physical in nature. Today, people do not seem to recognize their need for Him. But the truth is, we need Him now more than ever. As the world continues to spin out of control, our eyes can be closed to the sin around us and in us. It is important that we recognize and stay in touch with our need for the Savior. For there is no need to run after someone who can heal a disease that we are not even aware we have.

~ 15 ~

'These people honor me with their lips, but their hearts are far from me. Their worship is a farce, for they teach man-made ideas as commands from God.' —Matthew 15:9 (NLT)

Read Matthew 15:1-9

It is easy to click our tongues at the Pharisees. We have Jesus' words to show us the errors they committed. But are we guilty of doing the same things? Do we get mired in traditions and rituals that are contrary to God's word? In some cases, God will send people into our lives to point out these errors but, in truth, it is our responsibility to examine our lives daily in light of His scriptures. By doing so, we can continue to weed out the things in our lives, even things we have done for years that are contrary to what God ordains. We should continue to look in the mirror of the Bible frequently and remove that which is contrary to God's teachings. As we do, the old, earthly people will disappear and the children of God that we will become will be revealed to us.

~

Then the disciples came to him and asked, "Do you realize you offended the Pharisees by what you just said?" –Matthew 15:12 (NLT)

Read Matthew 15:10-14

There are going to be those who simply will not listen. In fact, some will be downright insulted that we said anything in the first place. But that does not relieve us from the responsibility of telling them about the Gospel in the first place. Once we have shared the Gospel, what they do with the information is up to them. But one thing is for sure. They will never have the excuse again of not knowing. So do not turn away from the opportunities presented to share what we know about Jesus Christ. Whether they are offended or not, those who receive the information will never be the same.

~

"Anything you eat passes through the stomach and then goes into the sewer. But the words you speak come from the heart—that's what defiles you." – Matthew 15:17, 18 (NLT)

Read Matthew 15:15-20

Just as the eye is the way we see the world, the tongue is the way the world sees us. We can act contrary to our nature for short periods of time, but sooner or later our words will betray our true selves. We try to filter our speech but our filtering is a conscience effort that will fail us at the worst possible moment. When it does, our true thoughts will roll right off of our tongue before we realize what we have done. That is why it is so important for us to tend to the real issue, our heart. The heart is, well, the heart of the problem. The heart is where the person we truly are, good and bad, resides and that person will find its way into the light through our tongue. This is why it is so important, for each of us, to find, and build, on our relationship with Christ. It is only through fellowship with Him, through believing in Him, and through surrender to Him that the person who lives in our heart can truly be changed. Then we will no longer have to worry about what the world sees through our tongue.

~

Jesus responded, "It isn't right to take food from the children and throw it to the dogs." She replied, "That's true, Lord, but even dogs are allowed to eat the scraps that fall beneath their masters' table." —Matthew 15:26, 27 (NLT)

Read Matthew 15:21-28

Are we humble? Are we humble to the point we would dare to compare ourselves to four legged creatures? This woman knew trying to measure up to those who were turning her away was not going to win her an audience with Jesus. She also knew an audience, and nothing less, would save her daughter. So she agreed with their assessment of her status and bent her neck instead of stiffening it. She got down on all fours like the dog she was being compared to and pointed out that even the dog receives compassion from its master. For her humility, she received the life of her daughter. What is it we seek today? Whatever it is, let's seek it on our face. No matter how good we are, we will never measure up. So we had better kneel down.

~

They laid them before Jesus, and he healed them all. –Matthew 15:30 (NLT)

Read Matthew 15:29-31

Do you know someone who is ill? Whether the problems are physical, emotional, or spiritual, we all know someone who needs healing today. We have the same opportunity to lay our loved ones at Jesus' feet as those who did so thousands of years ago. When we bend our knees in prayer, we can take our loved ones to the cross with us. Even if those we care for refuse to go willingly, we can still lay them at Jesus' feet when we meet Him in prayer. When we do, we will experience the same amazement that comes from acting in faith and seeing Jesus at work. Then we, like they, will have yet another reason for giving praise to our Heavenly Father.

~

Then Jesus called his disciples and told them, "I feel sorry for these people. They have been here with me for three days, and they have nothing left to eat." –Matthew 15:32 (NLT)

Read Matthew 15:32-39

Jesus repeatedly showed His ability to take care of those who followed Him. But notice that the primary concern was the people's spiritual well-being. Only after those spiritual needs had been taken care of, did He address their physical needs. Make no mistake, Jesus is concerned about our physical needs (not wants), but He is far more concerned about our eternal soul than our temporal bodies. This may sound harsh, but He is looking at things from a much different perspective than you and I. It is right and good that we trust Him to know what we need the most. Remember, He earned that trust when He gave Himself up on the cross to save us in the first place.

~ 16 ~

"Only an evil, adulterous generation would demand a miraculous sign, but the only sign I will give them is the sign of the prophet Jonah." —Matthew 16:4 (NLT)

Read Matthew 16:1-4

As usual, the religious leaders got it backwards. They went to Jesus and demanded a miracle before they would believe Him. But that was not the way He was working. Jesus was healing those who came to Him in faith; not so they would believe, but because they already believed. Those who demand the miracles first are only burying their heads in the sand because evidence of His authority is everywhere. It is visible for any who are truly seeking Him. So let's settle the question of our own faith. With the evidence available to us, we have no need for any more proof. We just need to believe.

~

So again I say, 'Beware of the yeast of the Pharisees and Sadducees.'" Then at last they understood that he wasn't speaking about the yeast in bread, but about the deceptive teaching of the Pharisees and Sadducees. —Matthew 16:11, 12 (NLT)

Read Matthew 16:5-12

Not much has changed in two thousand years. The Pharisees were pushing the same message that swirls around us today. The message is that you must save yourself. It is a message that rings true with humans because it plays to one of our basic emotions...pride. That is why it so easily permeates our society. It makes us feel good to think that we can work our way anywhere. School, the job, that house, and even Heaven are attainable for those who are willing to work hard enough. Every religion teaches this belief, except one. This is why Jesus warned the disciples about the Pharisees teaching. The Pharisee's message was in direct contrast to what Jesus was leading people to. The truth is no matter what we do, we will never be able to work our way out of sin. Our efforts might bring a degree, a better home, or even a dream job. But those efforts will never bring us to Heaven. We need help to reach heaven. We need a Savior. Let's pray more will come to understand the message of work for the lie that it is; and the only path to Heaven is through the Cross, where Jesus did the work that we never can.

~

Then he asked them, "But who do you say I am?" —Matthew 16:15 (NLT)

Read Matthew 16:13-20

Jesus' question is one we all, at some point in our lives, must wrestle with. Who do we say He is? Many have said He was a good man, or a great teacher, or even a prophet. Others question whether He existed at all. The truth is there are only three conclusions you can come to if you answer the question honestly. If you read the scriptures, you know Jesus, Himself, claimed the label Peter gives Him in this passage. For Jesus to say He was the Son of God could only mean that He was a liar and a con man, He was someone who was mentally unstable, or He was, in fact, the Son of God. There is no room to conclude He was only a good man or a prophet. He does not make our decision easy and He never intended intend to. But once the question is settled, we are ready to walk the journey of faith. Let's pray for those who still do not know Him. Let's also pray as people come to know Him, through God's word, that they settle not only the question of who Jesus was but also what He did for them.

Jesus turned to Peter and said, "Get away from me, Satan! You are a dangerous trap to me. You are seeing things merely from a human point of view, not from God's." –Matthew 16:23 (NLT)

Read Matthew 16:21-23

Peter, like so many of us, received a little insight and it immediately went to his head. One minute he was confessing Jesus was God and the next minute he was trying to counsel Him. The problem was Peter, like so many others of his day, did not understand the true mission of the coming Messiah. Are we not the same way? On those rare occasions God chooses to reveal to us how He is working in the world, it should humble us to know He has done so. Unfortunately, more often our newfound knowledge causes us to be "puffed up". This is why it is so important for us to stay under the direction of the Holy Spirit. On our own, we will always go in the wrong direction. Remember, we should receive revelation from the Father in deep humility. It is not given to us so we may be magnified, but rather so He will be glorified.

~

"If you try to hang on to your life, you will lose it. But if you give up your life for my sake, you will save it." —Matthew 16:25 (NLT)

Read Matthew 16:24-28

What are we willing to give up in order to save our own life? What is our soul really worth? These are important questions most of us, unfortunately, give very little consideration. The sad fact is intangible things in our lives are given less and less consideration in our increasingly materialistic world. This is why Jesus' words are more relative now than when He spoke them. What will you have to give up to follow Christ? I do not know. You may have to give up everything. You may be asked to give up nothing. You may fall somewhere in between. The critical piece is that we decide in our hearts, what we are willing to lose, before the question is asked. We should begin now to dwell on those unseen things that are of the utmost importance. For nothing is more important than our soul, or the life that is ours to lose.

~ 17 ~

But even as he spoke, a bright cloud overshadowed them, and a voice from the cloud said, "This is my dearly loved Son, who brings me great joy. Listen to him." —Matthew 17:5 (NLT)

Read Matthew 17:1-8

When we find ourselves in the presence of God, the best thing we can do is nothing. There is no need for talk, no need for action. When we find ourselves in His presence, we can be relatively sure we are not there because of something we did. So, why do we think we need to do something once we are there? No, the best thing we can do is simply experience His presence and listen for His voice. So let's do just that, and enjoy His presence for the blessing that it is.

~

Jesus replied, "Elijah is indeed coming first to get everything ready. But I tell you, Elijah has already come, but he wasn't recognized, and they chose to abuse him. And in the same way they will also make the Son of Man suffer." —Matthew 17:11, 12 (NLT)

Read Matthew 17:9-13

The world is at odds with the gospel. Some people are opposed to the truth of Christ and will use any means, even violence, to stop it. Even in civilized countries, such as our own, the gospel is constantly attacked. Though the means to prevent Christians from sharing the gospel may not be as violent now as they are in other countries, they soon will be. That is what Jesus was trying to prepare the disciples for and the message is the same for us today. We must be prepared for the possibility that our faith will not hold when it happens. Jesus said the student is no better than the Teacher, so why should we be surprised when the world treats us just as badly as Jesus was treated. We should realize the truth about what awaits us as Christ's followers and face it in faith. The reward for doing so is life eternal in a place where nothing can ever hurt us again. The cost for not sharing the gospel is far worse than anything we will face for our faith.

~

Afterward the disciples asked Jesus privately, "Why couldn't we cast out that demon?" "You don't have enough faith," Jesus told them. —Matthew 17:19, 20 (NLT)

Read Matthew 17:14-20

Why is faith so important? Why does God require it before He will move mountains, or heal sick loved ones, or change someone's heart? What does true faith look like if the disciples did not even have enough to compare to a mustard seed? What about our own faith? Do we really have faith that God is who He says He is, that Jesus did what the Bible says He did, and that the Holy Spirit will do what Jesus said He would do? Some questions can only be answered inside our personal relationship with Jesus, because that relationship is where true faith starts. As we believe in Him for small things, He will reveal to us what He is capable of doing, so that we may grow in faith and witness more and more of His power. Along with our faith, our wisdom to know what is important and what is not will grow; so that, in addition to having the faith to obtain what we ask for, we have the knowledge to ask for things of true importance, like gifts that glorify God and turn people's hearts to Him. It all starts with our relationship with Jesus. Let's find time to start that relationship, renew it, or go deeper than we ever have before. A mustard seed is small but even it is not attainable if we are unwilling to start the journey.

~

After they gathered again in Galilee, Jesus told them, "The Son of Man is going to be betrayed into the hands of his enemies. He will be killed, but on the third day he will be raised from the dead." And the disciples were filled with grief. - Matthew 17:22, 23 NLT

It's easy to sit on this side of history and admonish the disciples for some of their actions. Should they not have had enough faith by this point in their ministry to believe that Jesus would rise from the grave? Should they not have understood by now that Jesus was not on earth to set up a physical kingdom? Maybe, just maybe they did understand all of this. Maybe the disciples understood everything Jesus had taught. Maybe the grief they felt was because Jesus had to die at all. Should we not grieve over Jesus' death as well? Shouldn't we be upset that Jesus had to suffer a violent death and even worse, physical and spiritual separation from God, because of us? Let's not forget the magnitude of what Jesus went through for us. Maybe then we will better understand why the disciples did what they did.

~

Jesus asked him, "What do you think, Peter? Do kings tax their own people or the people they have conquered? " "They tax the people they have conquered," Peter replied. " Well, then," Jesus said, "the citizens are free!"
—Matthew 17:25, 26 (NLT)

Read Matthew 17:24-27

Jesus knew the citizens of Jerusalem were being taxed unfairly. But Jesus' purpose on Earth was not to start a revolt against Rome or Jerusalem. His mission was to spread the gospel of the Kingdom of Heaven. Starting fights with tax collectors was not going to advance His cause. Instead, He decided to turn it into a teaching moment about God's provision. When Jesus left this Earth, He passed His mission on to us. One thing we need to do is ask ourselves as we go about our day how do our actions affect our ability to complete our true mission. Will the people we are trying to reach listen to us if we are antagonistic? Can we make any concessions that do not violate our own beliefs? If we, like Jesus, can bend on the things that do not violate His message, then the people we are trying to reach will be more open to listening to His message. It is called speaking the truth in love and it was modeled by our Teacher. Should we not practice it as well?

~ 18 ~

"So anyone who becomes as humble as this little child is the greatest in the Kingdom of Heaven." —Matthew 18:4 (NLT)

Read Matthew 18:1-4

Why are we, as a species, so obsessed about being first, being the greatest, or being the most powerful? Greed and pride are very powerful and controlling emotions, but it takes us a while to grow into them. When we were children, none of us were trying to climb the corporate ladder, ascend to political office, or rule the world. No, back then we were innocent and dependent on parents who we trusted to know and take care of our needs. We were not looking to dominate other kids in the sand box. We just wanted to spend time with them. We trusted our parents and loved them and we loved others. Jesus' point was that we must, like the children we once were, trust the Father to provide for us. We must love Him and others. Through the help of the Holy Spirit, let's move past the grown up emotions of greed, pride, and selfishness to experience the relationship we can have with God when we approach Him with childlike innocence.

~

"Temptations are inevitable, but what sorrow awaits the person who does the tempting." —Matthew 18:7 (NLT)

Read Matthew 18:5-7

Apparently there is something worse than being lost in our own sin. For those who align themselves with Satan in his attempt to convince others to travel the super highway to hell, a special punishment is waiting. Our own sin is bad enough because of its deception. It stands there and tells us we are not that bad because we can look at others who are worse. But in doing so, we follow the deception straight into the ranks of hell and lead others there as well. My prayer today is about that decision. Do we choose sin, where the inevitable path puts us square in the middle of those who work to swell the ranks (misery truly does love company). Or do we instead choose life? Do we take the off ramp onto the road less traveled, where sin is rebuked and the gospel is proclaimed so others may exit as well? The choice should be made wisely, because, for those that choose to stay on the highway, the tollbooth ahead is one that no one can afford...and no one can avoid.

~

"So if your hand or foot causes you to sin, cut it off and throw it away. It's better to enter eternal life with only one hand or one foot than to be thrown into eternal fire with both of your hands and feet." –Matthew 18:8 (NLT)

Read Matthew 18:8-10

Is there something in our life that is causing us to sin? Whatever the cause, we must strive to rid ourselves of it before it forces us off course. Whether it is the love of a possession, the self-satisfaction of a habit, or the desire for a destructive relationship, anything that leads us into sin leads us away from Christ. Anything that leads us away from Christ will also prevent our entrance into eternal life with Him. So, while we still can, we should look into our own lives and identify what sin stands between us and Jesus. Then, we should take steps today to remove it before it removes us from the future that awaits all who believe in Christ.

~

"And if he finds it, I tell you the truth, he will rejoice over it more than over the ninety-nine that didn't wander away!" —Matthew 18:13 (NLT)

Read Matthew 18:12-14

God cares about those who are lost. If He cares about them, should we not also care? Instead of condemning them or avoiding them, shouldn't we be praying for them and speaking to them about the gospel as opportunities arise? After all, we would still be in their number if someone had not done the same for us. Someone came looking for us instead of leaving us out in the cold. So let's be of the same mind and ask God to renew our hearts so that we share His desire for those who do not yet know Him. For if we join Him in His desire, we will share in His joy when the next sheep returns to the fold.

~

"For where two or three gather together as my followers, I am there among them." —Matthew 18:20 (NLT)

Read Matthew 18:15-20

Jesus promised to be there anytime we gather in His name. Whether we are worshiping, praying, or deciding civil matters between followers, if we gather in His name, seeking His guidance, in an effort to act as He would act, then He promised He would be there. Under His guidance and in His wisdom, decisions can be made and requests can be submitted that are not only acceptable, but binding both here and in Heaven. That is why Paul could later admonish Christians who went to a judge to settle disputes rather than handling the matter internally. What judge on earth is wiser than the Creator of the universe? So, when we have disputes, or requests, or concerns, let's gather together, not as a committee or a jury, but as sons and daughters of the living God. As we sit together in prayer, we will be joined by Wisdom Himself, who will guide us in whatever it is we seek.

~

"That's what my heavenly Father will do to you if you refuse to forgive your brothers and sisters from your heart." —Matthew 18:35 (NLT)

Read Matthew 18:21-35

It is no surprise that Jesus would follow a discussion about judging with a teaching about forgiveness. After all, His purpose for coming into the world was so people could be forgiven through Him. But, He warns us, forgiveness is not quick, easy, or optional. We will have to forgive, sometimes frequently, those who hurt us and we will have to forgive them from the heart, not the mouth. We may be tempted to ask if we have to forgive EVERY time, but in light of everything we need forgiveness for, the answer should be clear. Jesus put it a different way when He was teaching the disciples how to pray, "Forgive us our debts as we forgive our debtors". Do we want forgiveness from God that is spotty, or conditional, or tongue in cheek? My prayer is that we take to heart that we will be forgiven in the manner we forgive others and we let that knowledge change us into true children who watch the Father at work and try to do the same.

~ 19 ~

"Not everyone can accept this statement," Jesus said. "Only those whom God helps." —Matthew 19:11 (NLT)

Read Matthew 19:1-12

Once again the religious leaders tried to trap Jesus into contradicting scripture, and once again He turned them on their ear. The religious leaders thought their memorization of scripture made them superior to anyone else, including Jesus. But Jesus shows us that knowing scripture is only part of it. Understanding what the scripture says is just as important. Study and prayer, while being guided by the Holy Spirit, will bring us to that understanding, but we must walk in humility. The Pharisees used their knowledge to place themselves above others. I pray that as we study God's word and ask the Holy Spirit for understanding, we find ways to use what we learn to help others in need and spread the message of the grace found in Jesus Christ.

"For the Kingdom of Heaven belongs to those who are like these children."
—Matthew 19:14 (NLT)

Read Matthew 19:13-15

More than once Jesus used the example of little children to explain the kind of faith it takes to come to Him and to believe in Him. Just as an innocent child trusts in their parent to provide for them and protect them, so should we lean on Christ for the protection He provides through salvation. If He saves us, should we not also trust Him to provide for us? But we cannot approach such faith while wearing the pride and the cynicism the world teaches us to don. We must divest ourselves of such garments and instead approach the throne in humility and belief. Then we, like the children, can receive the blessings of knowing Christ.

~

Someone came to Jesus with this question: "Teacher, what good deed must I do to have eternal life?" —Matthew 19:16 (NLT)

Read Matthew 19:16-22

What is it in our life that keeps us from following Christ with all of our heart? For some it is a job. For others it is a possession or possessions. Still others are held back by a relationship. We become so focused on what is happening in the here and now that we lose sense of all we give up in our eternal future. We must settle the question in our own hearts about what we are willing to leave behind so we can pursue Jesus. He may or may not ask us to let it go, but we must be ready just the same. Whatever we give up in this life so we may hold on to the Lord pales in comparison to what we will receive in the future. Any sorrow over loss will soon be forgotten in the joy that comes with everlasting life with the Father. Let's find strength in our faith for tomorrow, to let go of what is hindering us today. Better for the sorrow of temporary loss today, than the permanent variety, suffered by the young rich man, at having passed on eternal life in the glory of God.

~

The disciples were astounded. "Then who in the world can be saved?" they asked. —Matthew 19:25 (NLT)

Read Matthew 19:23-26

Who in the world CAN be saved? The truth is that no one can be saved without God's intervention. He provided that intervention in the form of a sacrifice. But even those who believe in Christ and His sacrifice do so only because they have been given the gift of faith. We cannot work our way to that point, think ourselves into it, or buy ourselves a spot. Humanly speaking, it is impossible to get there on our own. But with God, everything is possible. If we get on our knees and ask, He will give us the gift of faith. And through faith in the work of Christ on the cross, we can be saved. But we must be willing to ask and willing to accept, because our willingness is the only thing we have to offer.

~

Then Peter said to him, "We've given up everything to follow you. What will we get?" —Matthew 19:27 (NLT)

Read Matthew 19:27-30

Peter definitely did not have trouble speaking his mind. But, thanks to him, questions we would like to have asked were answered. We may not want to admit it, but most of us have wondered at some point, "What's in it for us?" Jesus assured Peter, and us, that anyone who chooses Him over the things of this world will receive so much more. They will receive eternal life. If someone stood before you, ready to give you a thousand dollars if you gave up the ten in your pocket, would you take it? In addition to salvation, Jesus has promised other rewards for following Him as well. My prayer is that we believe His answer to Peter and act on our belief. If we follow Him sacrificially here, we will want for nothing in eternity.

~ 20 ~

"When they received their pay, they protested to the owner, 'Those people worked only one hour, and yet you've paid them just as much as you paid us who worked all day in the scorching heat.'" —Matthew 20:11, 12 (NLT)

Read Matthew 20:1-16

Some people come to know and accept Christ into their lives at a very early age. Others do not find Him until their waning years. There is a temptation for those that believe early in life to look down on those who do not and a temptation for those who are late to the table to worry about what they may have missed. Christ's message is that the reward of salvation and everlasting life is the same regardless of when in life you asked Him into your heart. We all make that decision at the precise time God has planned for us. So we should not worry about what might have been or who was first. We should also not use it as an excuse to wait, for no one knows what the next year, the next day, or even the next hour will bring. So let's be joyful that we know Christ, regardless of when it happened. And for those who do not know Christ, let's pray that they come to know Him today, while there is still time. The reward is the same, no matter when you claim it. But you do have to claim it.

~

As Jesus was going up to Jerusalem, he took the twelve disciples aside privately and told them what was going to happen to him. —Matthew 20:17 (NLT)

Read Matthew 20:17-19

Now that we know the rest of the story, we may be tempted to read over this passage without much thought about it. But here Jesus is telling the disciples, in detail, what is going to take place in the near future. Did they understand, in that moment, that He was actually prophesying future events to them? Maybe. Maybe not. But the point of Jesus' words here was not so the disciples would know, ahead of time, what was going to happen. It was so they would know, after it happened, that He was who He really claimed to be. Jesus told the disciples about future events so that after His death they could have hope in His resurrection as well. He was trying to prepare them for His death by giving them something to hold onto after it had happened. He gave it to them so we would have hope as well. If He could tell the disciples ahead of time about His death and resurrection then should we not believe what He says about His return? Does that not give us hope as well? We may wonder at the despair of the disciples between Good Friday and Easter Sunday, but are we not just as guilty between His first coming and His second? My prayer as I write this is that we renew our hope by returning to the words of Jesus in the gospels. The road may still wind in front of us, but it does not mean that we cannot know who is at the end, and run to meet Him.

~

"For even the Son of Man came not to be served but to serve others and to give his life as a ransom for many." —Matthew 20:28 (NLT)

Read Matthew 20:20-28

Even the disciples fought through feelings of pride and indignity, worrying about such things as position and authority. But Jesus warned them, and us, that leadership in Heaven was completely different from leadership here on Earth. Here on earth, leaders are often those who fight their way to the top, stepping on both those who compete with them and those who cannot help them. In Heaven, leaders are those who kneel in order to give others a leg up, serve rather than wait to be served, encourage others instead of looking for their own praise. When we consider which kind of leader we are looking to be, we should first decide whether we are looking for others to praise us or for our Father in Heaven to reward us. When that is determined, we can pick up the mantel of eternal leadership and run with it.

~

Two blind men were sitting beside the road. When they heard that Jesus was coming that way, they began shouting, "Lord, Son of David, have mercy on us!" "Be quiet!" the crowd yelled at them. But they only shouted louder, "Lord, Son of David, have mercy on us!" —Matthew 20:30, 31 (NLT)

Read Matthew 20:29-34

Like the case of the blind men, the world is always admonishing those who call on the Lord. But those who refuse to be silenced, will be heard, because Jesus has a compassionate heart. His desire is that all would call on Him and find salvation. He will run to anyone who calls out to Him. So for those of us who are calling on the Lord, keep calling and do not stop. The world will do what it can to silence us, but if we persevere, we will receive the grace of God. And like the men without vision, we will be able to say that we were blind but now we can see.

~ 21 ~

This took place to fulfill the prophecy that said, "Tell the people of Jerusalem, 'Look, your King is coming to you. He is humble, riding on a donkey— riding on a donkey's colt.'" –Matthew 21:4, 5 (NLT)

Read Matthew 21:1-5

Matthew continues to show us how the Old Testament prophecy is fulfilled in the life of Jesus. Throughout his gospel, Matthew stays on track with his message to the Jews, showing them how Jesus is the only person in history who lived into the writings of so many prophets, hundreds of years before He was born. Men such as Moses, David, Isaiah, Jeremiah, and Ezekiel toiled at the pen, writing down what God gave them, about a person they never knew. Matthew had the privilege of showing how so many of those verses were brought to life in the Teacher from Nazareth. My hope is that reading his gospel will inspire us to go back and read those scriptures for ourselves, so we might see how those, and other scriptures, point out the truth; that Jesus was, and is, the Messiah.

~

"Who is this?" they asked. And the crowds replied, "It's Jesus, the prophet from Nazareth in Galilee." –Matthew 21:10, 11 (NLT)

Read Matthew 21:6-11

People can be very fickle. Here they are cheering for Christ and just a week later, many of the same people would be calling for His execution. Why? Because it turned out that Christ was not to become the kind of king that the people were looking for. They had allowed someone else, namely the Pharisees, to read and explain the scriptures to them. The religious leaders' misinterpretation of the prophets was passed on to the people because the people did not have the opportunity to study the scriptures for themselves. The people of Jesus' day may not have had that opportunity, but we do. When our faith is not firmly rooted in God's Word, we too can be swayed to another's way of thinking. That is why it is so important for us to study the scriptures and pray daily, because even we who profess Christ can be led in the wrong direction, if we are not diligent in our relationship with Him. We should always filter what others tell us through what we read in our bibles as we pray to the Holy Spirit for guidance. Otherwise, we too could be professing Jesus one day and crucifying Him the next.

~

He said to them, "The Scriptures declare, 'My Temple will be called a house of prayer,' but you have turned it into a den of thieves!" —Matthew 21:13 (NLT)

Read Matthew 21:12-17

The temple was supposed to be used exclusively for praising, and praying to, God. But over the years, it had transformed into more of a town square where everything except worship was taking place. We would have been more likely to see political discussions, tax collection, and commerce in the temple than collective praise. Is it any wonder that Jesus was upset? Would His attitude be the same if He walked into one of our churches today? If we truly are the body of Christ here on earth, then why is our attitude not the same as Christ's? God is not present simply because we erect a building and slap a sign on the front that says "Church". He only dwells where people are praising, and praying to, Him. Jesus knew that, so He went to work. So let's be like Jesus and commit to the hard work of turning our churches back to the worship of God. When we do, perhaps, we will see His presence in our churches as well.

~

Then Jesus told them, "I tell you the truth, if you have faith and don't doubt, you can do things like this and much more." —Matthew 21:21 (NLT)

Read Matthew 21:18-22

When we pray for something or someone, do we really believe we will receive what we ask for? Or, do we just hope we will? The difference is bigger than we may think. If we truly believe that God is real, that He loved us enough to send His Son to take our penalty, and that He is powerful enough to do anything, then why should we not believe that He is ready to do anything we ask for that is in agreement with His will? My prayer this morning is that when we ask, we believe that God is big enough to grant what we ask and wise enough to know whether or not we need it. Those who hope will often be disappointed. Those who believe never will.

~

"Did John's authority to baptize come from heaven, or was it merely human?" They talked it over among themselves. "If we say it was from heaven, he will ask us why we didn't believe John. But if we say it was merely human, we'll be mobbed because the people believe John was a prophet." So they finally replied, "We don't know." —Matthew 21:25-27 (NLT)

Read Matthew 21:23-27

People who refuse to believe in Jesus would rather say they do not know what is true, than admit who Jesus is. People who refuse to believe in a Creator would rather say everything happened by accident than admit we are put together too perfectly to not have a designer. Extraterrestrial planet seeding, long term evolution, and amoeba splitting lightning bolts are all unproven theories advanced under the same desperate logic as that of the Pharisees. Unbelievers would prefer to advance anything, no matter how wild or bad it sounds, as long as it is in opposition to the truth. How should we deal with this type of behavior? Just look at what Jesus did. He had already given them the truth so when they tried to argue with them He refused to engage. People who simply refuse to believe will not be won over by arguments. All we can do is present the truth of the gospel. I pray we have the courage to do just that and the strength to walk away from silly arguments over notions made up to reinforce the choice not to believe. With God's help, some of them will come to see how twisted their excuses are. And then they will need the seeds that we leave in their hearts.

~

Then Jesus explained his meaning: "I tell you the truth, corrupt tax collectors and prostitutes will get into the Kingdom of God before you do. For John the Baptist came and showed you the right way to live, but you didn't believe him, while tax collectors and prostitutes did. And even when you saw this happening, you refused to believe him and repent of your sins."
—Matthew 21:31, 32 (NLT)

Read Matthew 21:28-32

Do we speak about faith, or do we have faith? Do we profess obedience to God, or do we actually obey Him? Even if we, until now, have refused to obey, it is not too late to begin following Christ in action. But, for those who confess with their mouth and show something different with their actions, it would be better if they had never been born. Their actions betray the lack of faith in their hearts. So let's show our faith through our actions, as well as our words. Real actions back up real words and prove a real change of heart. And that is what real faith is all about.

~

When the leading priests and Pharisees heard this parable, they realized he was telling the story against them—they were the wicked farmers. – Matthew 21:45 (NLT)

Read Matthew 21:33-46

It is true that Jesus was referring to the religious leaders as He told this parable. But it is also true that it was meant as a warning to all who refuse to accept Him as God's Son. We have all been given custody, to some degree, of the vineyards waiting to be harvested. But we should remember that we are simply caretakers of the future harvest and not owners. Everything belongs to God, and at some point the Son who was murdered will return to remind us of that fact. How we treat those He sends for the harvest will determine how we will be treated. He will accept us only if we accept His Son. Will we be counted among those who accepted the Son with joy? Those who are remembered otherwise will never hear, or feel, the end of it.

~ 22 ~

"But when the king came in to meet the guests, he noticed a man who wasn't wearing the proper clothes for a wedding. ' Friend,' he asked, 'how is it that you are here without wedding clothes?' But the man had no reply. Then the king said to his aides, 'Bind his hands and feet and throw him into the outer darkness, where there will be weeping and gnashing of teeth.' "For many are called, but few are chosen." —Matthew 22:11-14 (NLT)

Read Matthew 22:1-14

Originally, God had invited the nation of Israel into a relationship with Himself. But over the centuries the Israelites mistreated those He sent to proclaim His word and they turned away from the invitation that God made to them. So He extended His invitation to the Gentiles (better known as everyone else) to come and know Him. Some, who accept His offer think they can approach Him while wearing the wrong clothing. You see, none of us, the rich or the poor, the wise or the foolish, the young or the old, can go to Him as we are, for the Bible tells us that all of our works are as filthy rags that we wear. Like the emperor in his new suit, we parade around in them like they are fine silk because we have convinced ourselves and others that they look so good. But there is only one gown that we may wear in the presence of God and that is the robe of righteousness we don when we accept Christ as our Savior. His work on the cross is the only work that is acceptable to God and those that answer the invitation must wear it or their time at the feast will end before it begins. So let's not fool ourselves by trying to slip into a relationship with God by any means other than the officially proclaimed invitation. The raiment has been provided. Not wearing it is a mistake that will cause us to miss the Guest of honor for eternity.

~

But Jesus knew their evil motives. "You hypocrites!" he said. "Why are you trying to trap me?" —Matthew 22:18 (NLT)

Read Matthew 22:15-22

The religious leaders could not have cared less about taxes or Caesar. Their praise of Jesus as a fair and honest teacher was not sincere either. They were simply trying to manipulate Him into doing what they wanted, giving them an excuse to arrest Him. Before we stand in condemnation of them though perhaps we should look in the mirror. Is our praise of God always sincere or do we sometimes heap praise because we are trying to sway Him? Are our conversations with Him always honest or do we find ourselves asking for something we do not care about simply because we think it makes us look good to Him? Do we express emotions that are not true because we are afraid to tell Him how we really feel? It is important for us to understand that God knows everything. Even when we convince ourselves about our intentions, we are not hiding anything from Him. That includes our thoughts, our motives, and our desires. Not only does He know them, He knows them before we do! So I pray that when we meet with Him, we are totally honest in our conversation. Even if we are upset with Him, it is better to be truthful. God is able to deal with anything we are going through and He is well aware of our problems long before we express them to Him. He can handle anything, as long as it is the truth.

~

Jesus replied, "Your mistake is that you don't know the Scriptures, and you don't know the power of God." —Matthew 22:29 (NLT)

Read Matthew 22:23-33

The Sadducees were a strange group. How can you have faith in God and not believe in His promises of resurrection? If God is not big enough or powerful enough to keep His promises, even those about life after death, then why bother believing in Him? That is what happens when, over time, we falter in the disciplines of study and prayer. Jesus told the group that they did not know the scriptures. When we fail to study, we lose our ability to think in light of God's word. He also told them they did not know the power of God. When we neglect our prayer life, we too lose our sense of who God really is, and how powerfully and wonderfully He moves in our lives. Trying to hold on to faith, when we allow the things of this world to keep us from study and prayer, turns us into empty shells, just like the Sadducees. So let's remain diligent in our walk with God so we have a faith that is living and powerful. For it really is sad, you see, to live like a Sadducee.

~

"Teacher, which is the most important commandment in the law of Moses?"
—Matthew 22:36 (NLT)

Read Matthew 22:34-40

You can search the entire Old Testament and you will never find a law that can be violated if you truly love God and love His creation... human beings... us. We cannot worship other gods if we love the one true God. We cannot kill, or steal from, or injure our fellow man if we really care about them. The problem is that when we do not love God and we do not love others then rules must be put in place to govern how we act. Israel had gotten so out of hand by the time they were banished to Babylon that those who later returned detailed the Levitical law to the nth degree in an attempt to force people not to sin. It was from these volumes that the Pharisees wanted Jesus to pick the most important law. But Jesus was having none of their shenanigans. If you distill everything down, all of the Levitical law and its Pharisaical addendum, you are left with love God and love people. Not a romantic love. Not a superficial love that says you do what you want and I will do what I want. A real love that knows God's heart, and wants what He wants. A love that cares about people and their future. A love that drives us to be as close to the Creator of the world as we can get. That was Jesus' point. When we love God, and others, with that kind of love it is impossible to sin against man, or God. And that is why love is the greatest commandment. As we draw nearer to the Father, and as we show true love for those He brings to us, we will begin to feel that love grow inside of us. And, as we grow in that love, we become more and more like Him.

~

Since David called the Messiah 'my Lord,' how can the Messiah be his son?" No one could answer him. And after that, no one dared to ask him any more questions. —Matthew 22:45, 46 (NLT)

Read Matthew 22:41-46

Paul called the Bible the sword of the spirit because anytime we find ourselves in a battle, it should be the first weapon we reach for. Even Jesus went to the scriptures whenever He was confronted, because there is no argument that can stand against them. The word of God is inspired, inerrant, and has the answer to any question we face if we are willing to search it with an open heart and a holy Counselor. Sharper than any physical sword, it can divide truth from error whenever it is used in its proper context. No matter what problem we face, we should always remember to unsheathe our sword before we turn anywhere else.

~ 23 ~

"And don't let anyone call you 'Teacher,' for you have only one teacher, the Messiah. The greatest among you must be a servant. But those who exalt themselves will be humbled, and those who humble themselves will be exalted." —Matthew 23:10-12 (NLT)

Read Matthew 23:1-12

Any position, whether it be religious, political, financial, familial, or volunteer can be a trap if it is approached with the wrong attitude. Most of the Pharisees had fallen into this trap, succumbing to the power and prestige of the office, and looking for the trappings that came along with their position. Pride will do that every time, if we are not careful. It will have us asking, "What is in it for me?", when we should be asking, "How can I help?" It will have us looking for what we can gain, instead of what we can give. But if we approach the things we do in humility, then our focus is on others instead of ourselves, and the desire for gain does not hinder the ability to assist. Our attitude is our decision, but Christ warns that whichever we choose now determines what we receive in the life to come. May I suggest we choose humility? For the rewards we might gain in the present pale in comparison to those of the future if only we have the patience that comes with the absence of pride.

~

"What sorrow awaits you teachers of religious law and you Pharisees. Hypocrites! For you shut the door of the Kingdom of Heaven in people's faces. You won't go in yourselves, and you don't let others enter either." — *Matthew 23:13 (NLT)*

Read Matthew 23:13-15

They say misery loves company and the Pharisees were a perfect example. Not only did they refuse the gift of life in Christ, but they did everything in their power to convince others not to accept it as well. They were blind to the true meaning of the Kingdom of Heaven and in their attempt to continue their traditions blinded others as well. Those who know the truth and deny it hurt themselves. But those who deny the truth and lead others away as well have reserved a special punishment for themselves. I pray none of us experiences that fate. Rather, I pray we all come into the light, and know the reward of leading others to Him, and to everlasting life.

~

"Blind guides! What sorrow awaits you! For you say that it means nothing to swear 'by God's Temple,' but that it is binding to swear 'by the gold in the Temple.' Blind fools! Which is more important—the gold or the Temple that makes the gold sacred?" –Matthew 23:16, 17 (NLT)

Read Matthew 23:16-22

The Pharisees were more enamored with the material trappings of their office than they were with the spiritual import of their calling and it showed even in the oaths that they took. Jesus was not condoning the practice of making oaths (He had already taught against the practice earlier in His ministry), but He was using it as an example of how far the religious leadership of Israel had gone off course. How were they to shepherd the flock if they could not even see that they had staggered into the ditch? It is a ditch, we too should be careful to avoid. There will be times we will be tempted to look around and count ourselves blessed, not by our spiritual position, but by the material things surrounding us. That kind of thinking can lead us down the path of making wrong decisions to hang on to our "stuff". The Pharisees themselves would soon become murderers, because they were afraid allowing Jesus to continue would mean giving up their authority and position. Let's not fall into the same trap. For the things of this world will not last no matter what we do to hang onto them. But, eternal life is just that, eternal, and the only way to lose that is by the choices we make.

~

"What sorrow awaits you teachers of religious law and you Pharisees. Hypocrites! For you are careful to tithe even the tiniest income from your herb gardens, but you ignore the more important aspects of the law—justice, mercy, and faith. You should tithe, yes, but do not neglect the more important things. Blind guides! You strain your water so you won't accidentally swallow a gnat, but you swallow a camel! - Matthew 23:23, 24 NLT

Following the rules had become the religion of the Pharisees. They were so focused on making sure they followed even the tiniest of laws that they forgot what the Law was really about. It is important that we obey God's commandments, but we must not forget they are there to show us we should love God and care for each other. Justice for the oppressed, mercy for those who stumble, and faith in God who loves us are the actions that fulfill the law. When we do these things with God's love in our hearts, we cannot help but follow the rules. We should worry less about the gnat and more about the camel. If we take care of the important things, the lesser things will fall into line.

~

"Outwardly you look like righteous people, but inwardly your hearts are filled with hypocrisy and lawlessness." –Matthew 23:28 (NLT)

Read Matthew 23:25-28

Jesus was really taking the Pharisees to task about the pains they took to make sure they looked good in front of others. They wore the right garments, hung out in the right places, and spoke the right words; all in order to give the appearance of being spiritual. The problem with appearances is that while they may work with people, they will not hide our soul from God. He is not fooled by the clothes we wear or the things we say. Our lives are an open book to Him so we might as well act the way we feel. How do we clean the inside of the cup? The same way we clean the outside. Just like we use a mirror to make sure our physical appearance is okay, we use one to make sure our spiritual condition is also. That mirror is our Bible. When we read it, and allow the Holy Spirit to speak to us, it will show us where we are lacking. If we allow Him, God will use the words to transform us from the inside out. When the transformation starts on the inside, it does not stop until our whole being has been made new. But none of that can happen until we have settled the matter of what we believe about Jesus. I pray that we recognize Him as Savior and accept Him into our lives. It takes all three persons of the Godhead to complete the transformation. But the change cannot start until we open the door to the One who stands outside and knocks.

~

"Then you say, 'If we had lived in the days of our ancestors, we would never have joined them in killing the prophets.' " But in saying that, you testify against yourselves that you are indeed the descendants of those who murdered the prophets." —Matthew 23:30, 31 (NLT)

Read Matthew 23:29-36

It is easy to say we will not be like those who have come before us. In reality, it is a lot harder to deny who we are. We look like, talk like, and even, to a certain extent, act like our ancestors. On our own, we will never fully out run the characteristics of our former family members, good or bad. Not unless we have help from a new family. God longs to be our Heavenly Father. He offered Christ, His first-born Son, so we could become sons and daughters as well. To those who accept the invitation, He sends the Holy Spirit to guide and to teach the ways of this holy family. We cannot change how we look or how we sound, but, with the Holy Spirit's help, we can change how we talk and how we act. Let's seriously consider the consequences, good and bad, of whether we decide to join God's family or not. Following those who came before us and failed only has one outcome, and once it is here, there are no second chances.

~

"O Jerusalem, Jerusalem, the city that kills the prophets and stones God's messengers! How often I have wanted to gather your children together as a hen protects her chicks beneath her wings, but you wouldn't let me." –
Matthew 23:37 (NLT)

Read Matthew 23:37-39

Never doubt that what God really wants is for everyone to turn to Christ and be saved. But it must be the decision of each individual. God has given each of us the freedom to choose between right and wrong, good and evil, Heaven and hell, because a decision for Christ means nothing if it is not made freely. So my prayer is that we make our choice in the freedom given to us by God, but with the wisdom He provides as well. For all roads are open to us, but only One leads to life.

~ 24 ~

As Jesus was leaving the Temple grounds, his disciples pointed out to him the various Temple buildings. But he responded, "Do you see all these buildings? I tell you the truth, they will be completely demolished. Not one stone will be left on top of another!" - Matthew 24:1, 2 NLT

The disciples were looking at the history of the temple, but Jesus was looking at its future. The disciples were focused on the tradition of the building while Jesus was warning of things tradition could not prevent. Jesus was trying to prepare the disciples for what was coming, not to scare them or cause them to lose hope, but so when these things happened the disciples' faith would be strengthened and hope would abound. As we listen to everything Jesus has to say, I pray we too would have our faith strengthened. If we believe in everything He has already done, then we can have hope in what He says He will do, regardless of what comes between now...and then.

~

Jesus told them, "Don't let anyone mislead you, for many will come in my name, claiming, 'I am the Messiah.' They will deceive many." —Matthew 24:4, 5 (NLT)

Read Matthew 24:3-5

Before His return, Jesus predicted many would try to claim the mantle of Messiah for themselves. Many, He said, would be deceived and many have been. The results are pretty predictable as well for those who follow these pseudo messiahs. Disappointment, disillusionment, and death are the eventual outcomes as grand promises are made, and broken, of special status, secret knowledge, and ring side seats to Armageddon or special transportation away from it. How will we know when Christ, the true Messiah, has actually returned? We only need to look to God's Word for the answer. At His ascension into Heaven, angels told the disciples that just as He left (rising into the air) so would He return. Jesus Himself said that when He returned there would be no doubt, for everyone would know about it from the East to the West. No one will have to ask, "Is this Him?" because everyone will know in their hearts (even those who do not believe) Christ has returned. If we continue to study the scriptures and what they have to say about Christ's return, then they will give us hope in spite of everything we see around us. We have enough to worry about these days. But one thing we do not have to fear is missing Jesus when He returns.

~

"And you will hear of wars and threats of wars, but don't panic. Yes, these things must take place, but the end won't follow immediately." —Matthew 24:6 (NLT)

Read Matthew 24:6-8

Jesus continues telling the disciples about signs that will signal His return and the end of this world as we know it. Many have tried to use these signs to predict when that end will occur, but in doing so they miss the point. Jesus' words are both a message of hope and a warning. For those who know Him, seeing the signs played out in the world today gives us hope that we will soon be reunited with our King. For those who do not know Him, it is a sign that time is running out. Tomorrow has never been promised to any of us. As we witness the words from Matthew's gospel being played out on the world's stage, we have to know that tomorrows are becoming fewer with each new day. If we know Him, then we can look past the signs of the present to the hope of the coming future. And if we do not, let's take time today, while it still is today, to seek Him out so our hope can begin before our tomorrows run out.

"But the one who endures to the end will be saved." —Matthew 24:13 (NLT)

Read Matthew 24:9-14

Does any of this sound familiar? Christianity has become a dirty word in this country. Many have denounced the faith because it does not agree with the life they want to live. Sin has become not just commonplace, but, in many cases, part of the new morality. Many, who once professed to love the Lord, have turned away because it is not politically correct to do so. So why fight it? That is what the world wants us to ask ourselves. Why not make it easy on ourselves and just join them? Because we know what awaits those who make it to the finish line. Those who endure will be saved and those who do not will face a much different fate. So let's be faithful to keep that hope in front of us. Those who make it to the end will not only be saved, but will also help to spread the gospel to others as well. And the spread of the gospel is the key to shortening the time we must endure.

~

"So if someone tells you, 'Look, the Messiah is out in the desert,' don't bother to go and look. Or, 'Look, he is hiding here,' don't believe it! For as the lightning flashes in the east and shines to the west, so it will be when the Son of Man comes." –Matthew 24:26, 27 (NLT)

Read Matthew 24:15-27

There will be dark days before Christ makes His return. In fact, they will be so bad that no one would survive unless God shortens those days. Things will be so evil that some will believe anyone claiming to be Christ returned. There will also be no shortage of those making the claim, with the ability to perform miracles and display supernatural powers. Even those who believe will be fooled unless they remember Jesus' promise. When He returns there will be no doubt who He is. For everyone will see Him, from the east to the west, at the same time. That is why it is so important to stay diligent in reading the scriptures. Not only do they remind us of the hope to come, but they also give us the tools to know truth from deception. I pray that we study the scriptures daily and use them wisely.

~

"Just as the gathering of vultures shows there is a carcass nearby, so these signs indicate that the end is near." —Matthew 24:28 (NLT)

Read Matthew 24:28-35

There will be great mourning among the peoples of the earth when Christ returns. Because even though all will see Him and recognize Him for whom He is, not all will be leaving with Him. We all have a chance, during our life here, to decide to follow Christ and accept what He has done for us on the cross. But that window of opportunity is not open ended. For those who die without having settled that question, the opportunity has passed. For those who are living when Christ returns, the window closes as well on that day. There will be billions, on that day, who realize they are too late to enter the kingdom. Then all they will be able to do is await the fate that comes to those who refuse the grace of Christ on the cross. That is why Jesus gave us these signs to watch for. Not so we could predict when His return would be, but so we would realize how close His coming is and settle the question in our own minds before it is too late. My prayer is that each of us would come to grips with who

Christ is and what He has done to save us. Because the list of things in this chapter that have not happened is getting smaller every day.

~

"However, no one knows the day or hour when these things will happen, not even the angels in heaven or the Son himself. Only the Father knows." —
Matthew 24:36 (NLT)

Read Matthew 24:36-44

Even Christ and the angels are waiting for the day the Father says, "Go!" Why all the secrecy? Because true devotion is what the Father desires from His children. How true is desire that is expressed only to escape punishment? If everyone knew the day of Christ's return, how many of us would do exactly what we wanted right up until that time, and then try to change our stripes at the last moment? No, God wants sincere followers who love Him for who He is, not for what they are running from. Let's look in our own hearts to make sure our devotion to the Father is real and true and, if He tarries, lifelong. If we are real with Him then, even as the world is going to hell, He will be real with us. And we will secure our place in Heaven.

~

"A faithful, sensible servant is one to whom the master can give the responsibility of managing his other household servants and feeding them. If the master returns and finds that the servant has done a good job, there will be a reward." —Matthew 24:45, 46 (NLT)

Read Matthew 24:45-51

Let's not be fooled into thinking that we, even as Christians, can put off our responsibilities until a later day. None of us know when our last breath will be and for us to say we will wait until a certain day to get serious about our duties shows arrogance we cannot back up. Those of us that have yet to decide for Christ cannot afford to delay that decision. And those of us who have decided abuse those who have not when we tarry in our responsibility to spread the Good News. For us to put things off until a more convenient day shows that we really do not believe God is who He says that He is. So let's carry our load while it is today. For tomorrow is promised to no one and the reward belongs to those who do not wait for it.

~ 25 ~

"But while they were gone to buy oil, the bridegroom came. Then those who were ready went in with him to the marriage feast, and the door was locked."
—Matthew 25:10 (NLT)

Read Matthew 25:1-13

We really cannot afford to be "halfway" Christians. We cannot be in love with the idea of being Christian then have our head turned by some other teaching or our attention diverted by some new pleasure. When that happens, scripture study stops, prayer stops, and ultimately faith grows cold. The danger is that once our lamp has gone out, then we are tempted to put off refueling. If the Lord returns before we have refueled, we are in grave danger of being left out in the cold. So let's not allow the trappings of this world prevent us from keeping our lamps filled. Let's stay in the word, continue in prayer, and keep serving. If we stay full and burning bright, we will be ready when He returns and we may just light the way for a few others.

~

" 'To those who use well what they are given, even more will be given, and they will have an abundance. But from those who do nothing, even what little they have will be taken away.' " –Matthew 25:29 (NLT)

Read Matthew 25:14-30

God has blessed us all with talents and abilities. What we do with them is a question He has given us the freedom to answer on our own. We can decide not to use them, we can use them for personal gain, or we can use them to spread the message of God's Kingdom. Whatever our decision may be, there will come a day when we will have to give an accounting of what we did with what we were given. On that day, the last thing we want to say is that we decided to nothing. Whether we were given the ability to speak, to serve, or to support, my prayer is we use those abilities to help bring others into the fellowship of Christ. After all, who doesn't want to be told, "well done," especially on that day.

~

"And the King will say, 'I tell you the truth, when you did it to one of the least of these my brothers and sisters, you were doing it to me!'" —Matthew 25:40 (NLT)

Read Matthew 25:31-46

James wrote in his epistle, "Faith without works is dead," and he challenged followers of Christ to display their faith through their works. What better way to display our faith than by loving God through the people He created? Caring for their basic needs allows us to partner with Him to perform the miraculous in their lives. More importantly, it changes our faith from rote ritual into active belief and reveals us to be sheep, instead of goats. Works cannot save us, but they do provide a barometer of the faith that does. Faith that does not result in obedience to the greatest commandment is about as genuine looking as a goat wearing a fleece in a flock of sheep. My prayer is that our genuine faith leads us into genuine concern for the people around us. The ones who were created by God, the same way He created us. When we do, our wool will grow thicker and our place among the sheep will be secure.

~ 26 ~

At that same time the leading priests and elders were meeting at the residence of Caiaphas, the high priest, plotting how to capture Jesus secretly and kill him. —Matthew 26:3, 4 (NLT)

Read Matthew 26:1-5

Pride. Greed. Arrogance. These sins caused a group of men to conspire against a teacher who was threatening their world. They thought they were protecting themselves from the impending discipline of Rome over another revolutionary who taught about a better kingdom. What they did not know was that their plans were not secret and they were unwitting pawns in a much greater plan to save the world. We make plans every day. Some are good and some not so good, but all are known to God. And, none succeed unless they are in accordance with His will and His plan. This may seem hard to believe given some of the things we see going on around us, but we are limited in what we see and what we comprehend. God is not. My prayer is that we make our plans in faith, and trust God when He changes them. If we do, our faith will grow and we will be ready when He presents us with new opportunities; even if they don't look like opportunities.

~

But Jesus, aware of this, replied, "Why criticize this woman for doing such a good thing to me?" —Matthew 26:10 (NLT)

Read Matthew 26:6-13

Even followers of Christ must be wary of having a critical spirit. Though we sometimes think we know what is going on, we simply do not know all of the circumstances. The disciples still did not fully understand what was about to happen and became indignant at the woman's actions. What are we tempted to become critical about? Do we really know all of the surrounding circumstances? Even when we are certain that we do, let's remember that the truth needs to be spoken in love. Do not forget that God has given each of us different gifts and He has called each of us in different ways. If we are true to that fact, then we have no reason to be critical, only caring.

~

Then Judas Iscariot, one of the twelve disciples, went to the leading priests and asked, "How much will you pay me to betray Jesus to you?" – Matthew 26:14, 15 NLT

Read Matthew 26:14-16

Some believe the reason Judas agreed to betray Jesus is because Judas thought that once arrested, Jesus would be forced to use His miraculous power to save Himself and usher in His kingdom. But whether Judas' betrayal was because he did not really believe Jesus would allow Himself to be put to death, or he did not believe Jesus was who He claimed to be, the bottom line is he just did not believe. When we say we believe, but we really do not, we leave ourselves open to wrong decisions, mistakes, and disobedience. It is so important that we settle this question of what we believe. It is the basis of everything else that we do in our life. We know how it ended for Judas. Only true faith will keep us from a similar conclusion.

~

Judas, the one who would betray him, also asked, "Rabbi, am I the one?" And Jesus told him, "You have said it." —Matthew 26:25 (NLT)

Read Matthew 26:17-25

Whatever Judas' motivation was for betraying Jesus, he surely did not expect his actions to be made public ahead of time. Imagine his surprise at being identified in front of the other disciples. But Jesus always knows what is going on in our lives. He will call us on it if we are willing to listen. Judas was not willing and he paid for that decision with his life. The cost is just as high for us when we refuse to heed the conviction of the Holy Spirit in our lives. God seeks to protect us from the consequences of our sin by troubling our spirit when we consider our actions. But only we can decide whether or not to heed the warning. As we listen for these warnings in our lives, I pray we will allow them to direct our actions accordingly. Warnings we encounter in our daily lives are put there for our protection. Warnings in our spiritual life are no different.

~

As they were eating, Jesus took some bread and blessed it. Then he broke it in pieces and gave it to the disciples, saying, "Take this and eat it, for this is my body." —Matthew 26:26 (NLT)

Read Matthew 26:26-30

Do you think the disciples had any idea while they were eating that meal what the next 24 hours would be like? If they had, would they have done anything differently? Maybe they would have listened more, or tarried a little longer, or clung to Jesus just a little tighter. At the time, they did not know the significance of that meal. But we do. When we participate in the remembrance of it, what is our attitude? Do we approach with reverence? Do we dwell on what it represents? Do we cling just a little tighter to Jesus as we participate in the meal that He started? However we celebrate the Lord's supper, let's make sure it is with an attitude of respect and reverence for what it represents and Who it celebrates.

Peter declared, "Even if everyone else deserts you, I will never desert you." Jesus replied, "I tell you the truth, Peter—this very night, before the rooster crows, you will deny three times that you even know me." –Matthew 26:33, 34 (NLT)

Read Matthew 26:31-35

No one likes to think that they will run when faced with adversity. We all want to believe, when the time comes, we will be able to stand up for our faith. But we should be careful about saying what we will, or will not, be able to do in the future. Even when Jesus quoted the prophet's foretelling of the disciples' abandonment, Peter insisted that He would not be among them. One problem with bravado is that it is pride-based sin. The other is that it is often followed with a generous helping of crow. My prayer is that when we see adversity coming in the distance, instead of bragging about what we will do, we get on our knees and pray to the Father for guidance and strength to face it. Hundreds of years before Jesus and Peter, one of the kings of Israel put it this way, "A warrior putting on his sword for battle should not boast like a warrior who has already won" (1 Kings 20:11 NLT). Better to rely on the One who can see the future than to brag about what we will do when we can't even see all of the present.

~

He went on a little farther and bowed with his face to the ground, praying, "My Father! If it is possible, let this cup of suffering be taken away from me. Yet I want your will to be done, not mine." –Matthew 26:39 (NLT)

Read Matthew 26:36-46

Have you ever asked for something in prayer only to receive the answer, "no"? If you have, then you are in good company. Even Jesus, the Savior of the world, was told no when He asked to be spared from the suffering he was about to endure. We all ask for things that sound reasonable. But, for one reason or another, they are not in the plan that God has for us so we do not receive them. When He was facing complete separation from the Father, Jesus prayed He would not have to go through with it. God knew that answering Jesus' prayer would be contrary to His plan to save us and so Jesus' request was not granted. God told Jesus no for our sakes. Take heart when His answer is no and follow the example of Jesus. His request was sincere. But He understood what the answer might be and committed to follow God regardless of the outcome. If we truly trust the Father, then let us make the same commitment. He knows what is best and He will carry us through whatever He carries us to.

~

So Judas came straight to Jesus. "Greetings, Rabbi!" he exclaimed and gave him the kiss. Jesus said, "My friend, go ahead and do what you have come for." —Matthew 26:49, 50 (NLT)

Read Matthew 26:47-50

Is it possible for someone who has truly accepted Christ in their life to turn around and betray Him? That question has been asked, and answered, through the ages. Was Judas ever a true follower? He walked with the group for three years, was one of those sent out to preach the gospel during Jesus' ministry, and, according to Matthew 10:1, had received power from Jesus to cast out demons and heal the sick. Some point to that and use it as an example to say that even those who do not truly believe can put up a good act. Others use it to point out that even the elect can be deceived by an angel of light. Whichever group you agree with, it points out the fact that we cannot afford to look at our relationship with Christ as a onetime event, where we accept Him and then do nothing else to further that relationship. He is not an acquaintance we meet once and then add to our list of friends without a second thought. If we are not careful to cultivate that relationship every day through scripture study and prayer, then we will make ourselves susceptible to attacks and subterfuge from Satan. Once he has a foothold, he will do everything he can to prevent us from seeking Christ's face. Even if we have drifted, it is not too late. We can do something today to move back into our relationship with Jesus. Given the strength of our enemy, the only defense we have is in the arms of the Savior.

~

"Put away your sword," Jesus told him. "Those who use the sword will die by the sword. Don't you realize that I could ask my Father for thousands of angels to protect us, and he would send them instantly?" —Matthew 26:52, 53 (NLT)

Read Matthew 26:51-56

With all of the savagery that Jesus faced in the next 24 hours, it can sometimes be easy to forget that He submitted to it willingly. As He pointed out to Peter, He could have stopped it at any moment with one word to the Father. But Peter, like so many of us, believed it was up to Him to defend Jesus and force events down what he thought was the right path. Even today, the temptation is to look at the events surrounding us and think that forcing people, groups, and countries down a certain path is the answer. But the truth is that if we do not believe God has the ability to work His plan, to work behind the scenes, to bring about His plan in His own way, then maybe we have missed the point of what it means to be a Christian altogether. It is one thing to follow Christ and offer the Gospel to others for their consideration. It is another thing entirely to take matters into our own hands and force people to act and believe like we do. We should do everything in our power to, in word and in deed, spread the Gospel of Jesus Christ. But then let's complete that action by believing in the Father to grow the seed and work His plan. It worked for our salvation. It will work for others' as well.

~

Then the high priest said to him, "I demand in the name of the living God—tell us if you are the Messiah, the Son of God." Jesus replied, "You have said it. And in the future you will see the Son of Man seated in the place of power at God's right hand and coming on the clouds of heaven." –
Matthew 26:63, 64 (NLT)

Read Matthew 26:57 68

Jesus plainly told the priests who He was and they made their decision about what to do with that information. That same decision confronts everyone. When we come to the point in our lives where we realize who Jesus Himself claims to be, we must make a decision. We must decide whether we are going to accept or reject who He is and what He has done. One decision leads to eternal life, while the other leads to eternal despair. No one can choose for us, but to ignore the question is to choose in absentia. We must choose wisely, for, in this matter, once our time is up there is no undoing a wrong decision. And we will deal with the consequences forever.

~

Suddenly, Jesus' words flashed through Peter's mind: "Before the rooster crows, you will deny three times that you even know me." And he went away, weeping bitterly. —Matthew 26:75 (NLT)

Read Matthew 26:69-75

Peter was so sure he alone would stand by Jesus no matter what. But the problem with we humans is we do not have the capability to see into the future. So for us to brag about what we will or will not do is not only arrogant but sin as well. When faced with the very real possibility of winding up on a cross next to Jesus, Peter's strength failed him and he fled before the crowd's accusations. We take Peter to task for not standing strong, but how much does it take to cause us to waffle? Peter was facing loss of life, but many of us cave in at the thought of loss of stature, loss of friends, or loss of family. Let's hold our tongue in discussions about what we would or would not do in given situations. Instead, let's pray to the Holy Spirit to strengthen us when those situations occur, and remember, that regardless of what the outcome may be, our Savior is not surprised. As Peter would later find, there is forgiveness for those who return to Christ, regardless of what we have done.

~ 27 ~

"I have sinned," he declared, "for I have betrayed an innocent man." "What do we care?" they retorted. "That's your problem." Then Judas threw the silver coins down in the Temple and went out and hanged himself.
—Matthew 27:4, 5 (NLT)

Read Matthew 27:1-5

Whatever Judas' original motivation was, he apparently did not think it would end in a death sentence for Jesus. Once the reality of his sin set in, Judas, like Peter, was convicted about his actions. But unlike Peter, Judas went to those he had been in league with to receive absolution and, upon getting none, lost all hope. When we place our hope in someone or something other than Jesus, we soon find that we are at the mercy of whatever we have placed our hope in. And, if there is no mercy there, it is not a far distance to the end of our own rope. When we have faith in Jesus, it does not mean that we won't have to deal with the consequences of wrong choices. Peter, like Judas, went through a period of conviction and remorse. But unlike Judas, he did not end it prematurely out of a sense of hopelessness. Rather, Peter held onto his faith, even in the dark hours and he received the forgiveness that comes for those who wait, with hope, on The Lord. I pray that even when we find ourselves in the dark times of our lives, we hold on to the hope of what lies ahead in Christ. The night is always darkest right before the morning. But the Son rise is sure to come!

~

This fulfilled the prophecy of Jeremiah that says, "They took the thirty pieces of silver— the price at which he was valued by the people of Israel, and purchased the potter's field, as the LORD directed." —Matthew 27:9, 10 (NLT)

Read Matthew 27:6-10

Hundreds of years before Jesus came in human form, a group of men, over just as long a time span, put pen to paper at the direction of the Holy Spirit and wove a tapestry about the life of the incarnate Christ. After Jesus' ascension, Matthew wanted to make sure the Israelites knew that His life was the only one that fit the predictions of their beloved prophets, so he took every opportunity to show them in the gospel he wrote. As in this passage, it is almost as though the prophets were recording history rather than predicting it. That is because God knows all, sees all, and plans all. Nothing, regardless of how small, goes on in this universe that surprises Him and all of it is happening according to the plan that He put into motion at the beginning of time. He put the stories of Jesus in the prophets' pens so the Jews would know when the Messiah had come. He also did it so we could look back and see how true He is to His own words. That way, as we see prophecy fulfilled, we also see that we can trust the promises of God. He gave up His own Son so we might be saved. He told everyone He would do it centuries before it happened. If He could do all of that, He can keep the promises He has made to us as well.

~

"Don't you hear all these charges they are bringing against you?" Pilate demanded. But Jesus made no response to any of the charges, much to the governor's surprise. —Matthew 27:13, 14 (NLT)

Read Matthew 27:11-14

Sometimes the best thing to say in a situation is nothing. There will be times in our lives when we are confronted by people who only want to make us look small, or themselves large. There will be times when we will be tempted to say things that will hurt the situation more than help. There will be opportunities to go beyond the truth with our words because the situation seems to call for more. My prayer is that in those times, we follow the example of our Savior. In humility, let's give only truthful answers, forgoing the temptation to embellish or go beyond the facts in order to impress. Then, having given an honest answer, let's reserve our speech and let God work in the situation. Remember the Creator of the earth resists those who are proud, but gives grace to the humble.

~

And all the people yelled back, "We will take responsibility for his death—we and our children!" –Matthew 27:25 (NLT)

Read Matthew 27:15-26

How could these people, who celebrated Jesus' entry into the city just a week before, be calling for His crucifixion now? It's simple, humans are fickle. If we are not careful, our heads can be turned by anyone with a convincing story. The Jews were no different. They made an important decision based on a story fed to them by someone else. God has blessed us with a record of His interaction with us and a Spirit to reveal the truths of that record. There is no reason to follow others blindly. He has given us these gifts and the faculties to use them when we judge what others tell us. The Israelites did not do that and wound up cursing themselves and their children. So let's stay grounded in God's word. That way when others come to us with convincing stories, we can make our own decisions, and will not make ones that our children will regret.

When they were finally tired of mocking him, they took off the robe and put his own clothes on him again. Then they led him away to be crucified. — Matthew 27:31 (NLT)

Read Matthew 27:27-31

Jesus experienced torture at the hands of the Roman soldiers that most of us cannot even imagine. But that was just a precursor to the real sacrifice He would make for each of us. Do we face persecution for our faith? Perhaps, but Jesus Himself told us that if we were going to follow Him, then we could expect to suffer at the hands of the world just as He did. When we do, we should hang on to the hope that He went through it first to show us that it is only temporary. And, if we are faithful, after we have shared in His temporary suffering, we will enjoy His eternal reward as well.

~

After they had nailed him to the cross, the soldiers gambled for his clothes by throwing dice. Then they sat around and kept guard as he hung there. — Matthew 27:35, 36 (NLT)

Read Matthew 27:32-44

It is safe to say that execution in Jesus' day could not be considered humane by any stretch of the imagination. Stripped of all His clothing, spikes driven through his wrists and feet to hold Him in place, and hung in the hot sun on a cross where He had to push Himself up for each breath. And, all the while, people were hurling insults at Him, laughing at Him, and fighting over His clothes. This, on top of the brutal treatment He received from the soldiers earlier, was more than you or I could ever hope to survive and yet the real sacrifice He made was still to come. The next time we are considering what it costs us to claim our faith in Him, we would do well to remember what it cost Him to claim us.

~

At about three o'clock, Jesus called out with a loud voice, "Eli, Eli, lema sabachthani?" which means "My God, my God, why have you abandoned me?" ...Then Jesus shouted out again, and he released his spirit. At that moment the curtain in the sanctuary of the Temple was torn in two, from top to bottom. —Matthew 27:46 & 50, 51 (NLT)

Read Matthew 27:45-56

At last, the real sacrifice had been made. The brutality, the crucifixion, the insults of those who had once cheered Him were all painful, no doubt. Any one of those trials is more than we ever would want to go through. But, all of that pales in comparison to having the Living God completely sever His connection to you. We cannot understand that because, even though we may turn our backs on Him, He has never turned His back on us. God is still present and available to everyone through the Holy Spirit. Even people who refuse Him will not know what it is really like to be separated from Him, until their life in this world is over. At the moment of His death, Jesus, our perfect High Priest, offered the perfect sacrifice, settled the entire debt, and placed each of us who accept His sacrificial gift in a holy relationship with the Heavenly Father. That is why the veil was torn. Nothing would ever separate God from His people again, except their own sinful wills. Today, allow to sink in exactly what it is that Jesus gave up so we would never have to do so ourselves. Better to realize it now, than make the discovery in eternity. For once the relationship is gone, we will never get it back.

~

As evening approached, Joseph, a rich man from Arimathea who had become a follower of Jesus, went to Pilate and asked for Jesus' body. — Matthew 27:57, 58 (NLT)

Read Matthew 27:57-61

Even after His death, those who followed Jesus were willing to give what was theirs to honor Him. Joseph was a member of the Pharisees and stood to lose quite a bit by committing this act of love for someone the Pharisees had fought so hard to be rid of. Yet he and Nicodemus, another Pharisee, personally transported and prepared Jesus' body for burial. Why go through all of this for someone whose ministry was cut short prematurely? The answer is that they believed the rest of the story, even when it was yet to occur. Jesus promised that He was the Way, the Truth, and the Life, and even though they might not have known how, Joseph and Nicodemus were convinced the path Jesus laid out would not disappear. So, they put their own reputations on the line to continue honoring and following Him. My prayer is that we find the strength to follow their lead. We, like they, are in a season of waiting for Christ's return. Like them, let's continue to honor and follow Him until He does.

~

They told him, "Sir, we remember what that deceiver once said while he was still alive: 'After three days I will rise from the dead.' So we request that you seal the tomb until the third day. —Matthew 27:63, 64 (NLT)

Read Matthew 27:62-66

The Pharisees were so worried about the disciples trying to fool people that they defiled themselves by going to see Pilate on the Sabbath. It never occurred to them that Jesus might actually rise from the dead, so they concentrated their efforts on preventing any subterfuge. That is what happens when our faith is misguided. Our priorities become misplaced and we make wrong decisions. We become focused on trying to control things, thinking we can bring order to our own lives. We defile ourselves, we close our minds to the truth, and we find ourselves fighting God instead of seeking Him. Let's continue to root our faith in the Father, the Son, and the Holy Spirit. When we trust in them for our daily lives we will not find ourselves fighting against them for control.

~ 28 ~

"Don't be afraid!" he said. "I know you are looking for Jesus, who was crucified. He isn't here! He is risen from the dead, just as he said would happen." —Matthew 28:5, 6 (NLT)

Read Matthew 28:1-10

Jesus is risen! Why is that important? He promised that, as His followers, we would be resurrected just like Him. If He had been put in that grave and never heard from again, how could we believe in the promise? But He did rise and so we can have faith that we will do the same. His resurrection confirmed His sacrifice for our sins was valid and so we can have faith that our acceptance of that act makes us righteous before the Father. These two events are the bedrock of our Christian faith. If they had not occurred, then belief in the rest of it would be pointless. So my prayer is that we anchor our faith to the three words that give us hope. HE IS RISEN!

~

As the women were on their way, some of the guards went into the city and told the leading priests what had happened. –Matthew 28:11 (NLT)

Read Matthew 28:11-15

When we consciously decide to travel down the wrong path there is usually a "point of no return". If we continue to press on, it is impossible to get back to where we were before we made that decision. Once we pass that point, we find ourselves doing everything we can to justify those decisions and protect ourselves from the consequences. For the Pharisees, that point was the crucifixion of Christ, a person they felt would bring the wrath of Rome down on the country. Can you imagine the Pharisee's faces when they were presented with the soldiers' eyewitness accounts of the resurrection? They could no longer deny who Jesus was but neither could they return from the decision to kill Him in the first place. So they decided to cover their tracks instead. They concocted a story that the eyewitnesses observed the disciples stealing Jesus' body, and thereby attempted to cast reports of the risen Christ into doubt. Let's stay on course by staying in relationship with the Father and the Son through the Holy Spirit. It is inevitable that we will step off of the path at times, but as long as we follow the leadings of the Spirit we will always find our way back. If we neglect our relationship with the Holy Trinity, we will find ourselves covering our tracks as we wander further away.

~

"Therefore, go and make disciples of all the nations, baptizing them in the name of the Father and the Son and the Holy Spirit." —Matthew 28:19 (NLT)

Read Matthew 28:16-20

Everything Jesus did, the teaching, the healings, the miracles, and His sacrifice on the cross, is pointless if it ends with us. If we are now in a relationship with the Lord, it is because someone introduced us to Him. Whether it was a pastor, a preacher, a parent, or a friend, someone invested the time and took the risk to tell us about Christ, and explain exactly what He did for us on the cross. But Jesus' commandment was not to go and make disciples until you get to (insert our name here). No, Jesus wants all nations to know about Him. Now that we have entered into His family, He wants us to know the joy of bringing His story to others as well. As we leave the gospel of Matthew, let's reflect on the life of Jesus and what it has meant to us. If it has made any difference in our lives, how can we deny that same opportunity to others? God has gifted all of us differently so we can share His story in different ways, but always so we can share.

So let's find someone to share with, remembering that just as the commandment was meant for all who follow Jesus, so was the promise, "I am with you always, even to the end of the age."

~ What's Next? ~

Well that depends. If you already had a relationship with Christ before you began to read this book then my prayer is that walking through this devotional has somehow helped you to go deeper. I hope that it has helped you to realize the joy that comes from slowing down and spending time with the Holy Spirit as you allow Him to apply each scripture verse to your life. If this guide has done nothing more than help you to establish a regular time each day to meet with God then I join you in praising Him for it. If you find any of this to be true, I ask you to consider passing it along to someone else you know so that it may do the same for them. I ask also that you consider how God is calling you into the mission field. You do know that we are all called, don't you? Know that I am praying for you as you listen to His whispered summons, and consider how you might use the talents He has blessed you with to answer.

If you didn't know Christ before reading this, then I praise God for the person who gave it to you! I pray that, somewhere along the way, you have acquiesced to the invitation that the Father makes to all; to accept what the Son has done for us. You have probably figured out by now that it is not enough to know about Jesus. You must also *know* Jesus. For it is only in knowing Him that you will ever be able to receive the grace of accepting Him. And it is only in accepting Him that you will ever receive the gift of eternal life. Have you accepted Jesus? If you have, I rejoice with the angels in heaven at the regeneration of your spirit and the swelling of the family. I pray that you have found a loving church family in which to grow and learn. And I encourage you to continue in the daily study of God's word and the regular meeting with Him in prayer.

If you are still unsure about all of this, I want you to know that I pray for you as well. I ask you to remember this; God is big enough for your doubts! He is not offended when you take questions to Him. Confess to Him that you still don't believe. Ask Him to show you the way. It may feel awkward at first, given your misgivings. But if you sincerely seek answers from Him, He will be faithful to supply them. God's desire is that all would be saved, but He will force no one. It must be your desire to be saved as well. Once it is, confess your sins to Him and ask for His forgiveness. Accept His Son, Jesus, and exchange your filthy rags for a robe of white. Once you have, tell someone. The only joy that compares with receiving new life is sharing it with someone else. Find a church that preaches and teaches God's Word. Even the country road can be hard to travel alone. Find fellow travelers who you can share your experiences, and struggles, with. Email me at countryroad@cableone.net so that I can rejoice in your new life with you. And know that Christ is always with you, even to the end of the age.

Always remember this, interstate reading will get you the information faster but faster is not always better. I pray for all of you; that you continue to seek out the slow, quiet, intimacy of study and prayer; that you continue to grow in Christ; and that you continue to keep your sights set on our real home, where we will fellowship together forever. And I pray that until then, we keep helping each other as we walk the country road.

Watch for more devotionals in "The Country Road" series!!!

Visit our website at www.thecountryroad.net

Like us on Facebook!